LSAT
NECESSARY

AN LSAT PREP TEST GUIDE FOR THE
NON-LOGICAL THINKER

© 2016 by Aarambh Shah. All rights reserved.
First Edition, 2016.

99 PAGES OR LESS

Published by 99 Pages or Less Publishing, LLC
Miami, FL
For bulk discounts email: info@99pagesorless.com

Printed in the United States of America
10 9 8 7 6 5 4 3 2 1

Cover Design: 2 Faced Design
Copy Editor: Rachael Price
Index: Rosie Wood
Typesetting: Mandi Cofer

Library of Congress Cataloging-in-Publication Data is available for this title.
Library of Congress Control Number: 2016904536

ISBN: 978-1-943684-04-5 (hc); ISBN: 978-1-943684-03-8 (sc);
ISBN: 978-1-943684-05-2 (e)

Disclaimer: This publication is designed to educate and provide some general information on studying and preparing for the Law School Admissions Test (LSAT). It is sold with the understanding that neither the publisher nor the author is engaged in rendering legal, accounting, or other professional services. Further, the advice and strategies contained herein may not be suitable for your situation. Therefore, if you need legal advice or expert assistance then seek services of a competent professional.

Every effort has been made to make this manual as complete as possible and as accurate as possible. However, there may be some typographical mistakes and errors in content. Neither the author nor the publisher assumes any responsibility for any errors or omissions. Furthermore, the author and the publisher shall have neither liability nor responsibility to any person or entity with respect to any loss or damage caused, or alleged to have been caused, directly or indirectly, by the information contained in this book.

No part of this publication may be reproduced, stored in a retrieval system, or transmitted in any form or by any means, electronic, mechanical, photocopying, recording, scanning, or otherwise without written permission.

Dedication

To my brother, who taught me how to think about thinking without thinking.

"Education is the best provision
for the journey to old age."

—Aristotle

LSAT
NECESSARY

AN LSAT PREP TEST GUIDE FOR THE
NON-LOGICAL THINKER

ARAM SHAH

Contents

Foreword by Sapneil Parikh, DMD	xii
1. Introduction: Relearning How to Think	1
2. Lsat: Ready, Steady, Go	12
Finding the Truth (0-100)	12
Sufficiency vs. Necessity	16
Cause and Effect: "The Married Couple"	31
"The Home-Wrecker"	32
3. Logical Reasoning Is Selective Reasoning	36
Don't Get Lost in the Sauce	37
Common Argument Structures	37
Basic Argument Forms	39
The Olympic Long-Jumper	42
4. Deducing The Truth In Inferences	46
"All" Statements	46
MBT vs. CBT	47
MBF vs. CBF	48

"No" Statements	48
"Some" Statements	49
5. Closing the Gap: Finding the Assumption	**54**
Non-Related Arguments	54
Related But on Steroids	60
6. Passive Patterns	**67**
Conclusion Patterns	69
Spotting Conclusions Fast	73
Evidence Patterns	74
Valid Argument Patterns	76
Sufficient Assumption Patterns	78
The "U" Pattern	80
The Reverse "U" Pattern	81
The Block Method: "Some" and "Most" Statements	82
7. The Tricks of the Trade in Logical-Reasoning Questions	**90**
Seven Questions to Attack Logical-Reasoning Arguments	92
Seven Questions to Attack Logical-Reasoning Non-Arguments	93
How to Paraphrase Dense Arguments	94
Best Practices by Question Type: Non-Arguments	97
Best Practices by Question Type: Arguments	104
8. Reading Comprehension: Researching, Not Reading	**121**
The Purpose: Explain or Argue	123
How to Scan Keywords	123
The Most Important Question to Ask: Why?	124
The Push-Up Method	125
How to Take Notes	125
How to Predict	126
Don't Do the Questions in Order	126

The Three-Minute Rule	128
Mastering the Comparative Passage	129
9. Practice Makes Almost Perfect	**131**
The Six-Month Study Plan	132
The First Three Months	132
The Fourth and Fifth Months	132
The Sixth Month	134
Timing Strategy	132
10. Playing Games (Analytical Reasoning)	**137**
Multiple Sketches	137
Logic Games are Fun	139
The Fantastic Four	140
Ordering Games (sequencing, ordering, scheduling, ranking)	140
Grouping I Games (selecting, choosing)	143
Grouping II Games (distribute, accompany, form groups with 2+ entities)	149
Matching Games (distribute, accompany, form groups)	151
Hybrid Games (combination of actions)	153
Mastering Rules and Deductions	154
Attacking the Questions	157
Timing Strategies for Games	158
11. Perfect Practice: Scripts to Think	**160**
Logical-Reasoning Thinking Script (Argument Questions)	161
Reading-Comprehension Thinking Script	163
12. Check The Scoreboard: Bagging Points	**167**
The Million-Dollar Game	167
Treat the LSAT Like a Business	168

How to Get Faster	169
Scoring Strategy: Working Backwards	171
13. How To Review Your Practice Tests The Right Way	**173**
14. The 15-Point Triage Rule	**176**
How to Bag 15 Points in Reading Comprehension	177
Focus on Big-Picture, Detail, and Inference Questions	178
How to Bag 15 Points in Logic Games	181
Focus on the Single-Action Games	181
How to Bag 15 Points in Logical Reasoning	184
The Chunking Strategy	184
The Main-Point Mantra	185

Final Words	**189**
APPENDIX A: The Secret Language of Lawyers	**193**
APPENDIX B: Time-Draining Questions on the LSAT	**195**
APPENDIX C: Know Your Capabilities—Timing with Accuracy	**198**
APPENDIX D: Common Evidence and Conclusion Patterns	**200**
APPENDIX E: Logic-Games Homework—Practice Drills by Question Type	**204**
APPENDIX F: Reading-Comp Question Identification Types	**217**
APPENDIX G: Reading-Comp Structure Patterns	**220**
APPENDIX H: 25 Signs You're Ready to Sit and "Write" the LSAT	**224**
APPENDIX I: Common Wrong-Answer-Choice Traps in Logical Reasoning	**227**
APPENDIX J: Acceptance Letters	**229**
Index	**248**
About The Author	**259**

Acknowledgments

Many thanks to the University of Miami Friends of the Library Organization for allowing me to spend countless hours in the library, studying and preparing to write for the LSAT. The Otto G. Richter Library is an excellent resource for anyone who wants solitude to prep for this beast of a test, and always has a friendly and fantastic staff.

FOREWORD

When I was twenty-seven years old, I had just completed my higher-education degree and had missed my acceptance into professional school by a mere three points on a nationally standardized exam. I was horrified of having a precarious and unpredictable future ahead and that my path, and my dreams were all closing in. I had done so well in my master's program and maintained a full-time clinical position at my university that was also paying for my program. I was sure that I was one step closer towards fulfilling the "American dream."

The day when I found out that I missed the passing score on the national exam was probably one of the most humbling days of my life. After several days of grieving, I turned my anger and frustration into opportunity and focused on what I could do to help students to avoid the same challenges I had faced. Therefore, my lifelong mission was to teach students from an early age how to take standardized exams and think critically. In 2010, I launched Sapneil Tutoring Inc., a test-preparation company focused on helping the average-scoring student obtain success on all standardized exams.

I started training students, from those who desired to attend prestigious high schools across the nation to achieve high scores on high-school placement exams all the way to students who wanted to attend their dream undergraduate university. So naturally when I read this book, Aram's story and connection hit home, and I understood his vision not only to help the average-scoring student understand how to think logically through test prep, but also to provide the best tips/secrets that work when applied.

This book provides students who don't feel they were born with the intelligence or naturally acquired skills of being a good "test-taker" with the adequate skills and proper perception to outperform on the LSAT exam. There are a lot of good LSAT prep books out there, but Aram takes a bottom-up approach to understanding, analyzing, and mastering the LSAT. No doubt there will be long hours of preparation, but the choice to spend long hours preparing without any direction and individual goals are common pitfalls that students preparing for standardized exams fall into immediately. Aram provides long-term strategies that work to improve learning skills and achieve long-term success as a future law student.

As an education entrepreneur and full-time practicing dentist, I realized that testing was a rite of passage in my profession, so I decided not to take a laborious approach to achieving and beating standardized tests. During dental school, I had to take over seven long exams, ranging from the state law exam, which was one eight-hour test, to the state board exams, which involved three consecutive days of testing (for at least eight hours each day). Like the practical study habits I implemented, the fundamental test-taking strategies to do well on your LSAT are all concisely presented in this book and will help the non-logical thinker understand, interpret, analyze, and evaluate the steps to think logically.

In sum, I would advise setting measurable goals, studying efficiently, and staying determined. Most importantly, let Aram be your coach through this long journey. I wish you all the best, and hope to hear that each one of you cross that finish line and achieve that Juris Doctorate!

Sapneil Parikh, DMD, MS, MPH
Founder of Sapneil Tutoring Inc.
www.sapneiltutoring.com

1

INTRODUCTION: RELEARNING HOW TO THINK

The first time I opened up a study guide for the Law School Admissions Test (LSAT), I was petrified. It was like I was reading a textbook in a foreign language. Coming from a business and marketing/sales background, I knew very little about logic. In fact, I would now argue that I was an expert in logical fallacies. This was proven by my failed attempts at answering LSAT questions correctly over and over again. After starting, scaling, and selling several small businesses, I realized that the LSAT was the most challenging (and humbling) experience I had ever faced. At times I wanted to quit. However, my desire to move on from my current career path was so great that it overrode my fear of failing.

In 2015 I sold my successful real-estate brokerage firm to

pursue my dream of becoming an attorney. Passing the age-30 milestone I knew I had one more run, a chance at a second career, and the first step to gaining a seat in law school was conquering the LSAT. Plus, with law-school application rates at nearly all-time lows, it was now or never.

I took my first real LSAT on October 3, 2015. I remember that day as if it were yesterday. There were about 150 students at the test center, of which groups of about 50 were broken up into different classes. The silence just prior to the test was frightening and the anxiety levels were high. The proctor, prior to beginning, tried to lighten up the mood with a joke, but it was to no avail. I remember that, as soon as the proctor said, "Start," I opened up my first section and saw that it was logical reasoning. I was like, "Okay, I got this"; prior to testing I had taken approximately eight full-length practice tests.

As I started working through the questions I noticed my neighbor scribbling profusely. I thought, "What is this guy doing?" and then realized that he was doing logic games while I was on logical reasoning. That completely threw me off, especially since I had done all my self-study in a library with little to no noise. As I started working through the questions I kept on rereading each stimulus and all the corresponding answer choices. By the time I completed 12 questions (out of 26), there were five minutes remaining on the clock. What a horrible feeling.

About three days after the actual test, I decided to cancel my score. I knew as I finished the exam that there was no chance of my achieving my target score of 150. After hiding under a metaphorical rock for two weeks, I emerged determined to maximize my potential. I knew that I understood the abstract concepts; it was just a matter of applying them in a timed environment. So, off I went. I refused to fold.

I rigorously approached every single question type with a specific strategy and the second time around I worked twice as much on timing drills as on fundamentals. I noticed my practice test (PT) scores slowly jumped from the mid-130s to the mid-140s and eventually into the 150s. Thus, after 480 hours of intense practice, I retook the LSAT in December 2015. In contrast to the October 2015 exam, I kept on telling myself, "All I need is 15."

Yes, I forced myself to focus on small, minute goals and I ended up seeing a 15-point gain. Not bad for not even knowing what an assumption was six months prior. I worked very hard. I put in the time. I was literally relearning how to think (as the test-makers want you to).

The beautiful thing about this standardized test, which I eventually discovered, is that it can be beaten. Everyone gets it eventually: some people take two months; some take 12 months. It takes time to internalize the material. After a while your mind starts seeing patterns, just as you would when going to the gym every day. You could probably guess, depending on what time it was, who would be outside and which employee would be working.

Similarly, when tackling an LSAT inference question, you know what the wrong answers will look like (i.e., they bring in outside information not mentioned in the passage) and know how to solve for the correct answer. The same goes with assumption questions, for which the wrong answers typically restate a fact mentioned in the stimulus that obviously can't be an assumption, because an assumption is, by definition, an unstated piece of evidence. It's just a matter of time. If you stick with studying and practicing the material long enough you will more than "get" the LSAT—you will master it.

Why is time the answer? Well, the questions are basically all the same, structurally speaking. The only variation is the context. They have to be this way—it's standardized. The only major difference between two test-takers (who study and prep for the same amount of time) has nothing to do with the test itself, but rather with their natural abilities. Everyone comes to the LSAT table with different vantage points. This makes sense. Not all bachelor's degrees and high schools are the same. Some people have been taught to think critically since the age of three by their parents or their private school and others, like myself, have not.

This is ultimately measured by your initial LSAT attempt: your first full-length practice test. Mine, as a non-logical thinker, was a 136. Some people may take it the first time around with no prep and score a 150. It doesn't matter. What's important to remember is that, with hard work and dedication, you are capable of seeing at least a 10 to 15-point gain no matter where you begin on the lower end of the LSAT score distribution (The full score range is 120 to 180). However, you must become an LSAT connoisseur and see enough problems to know what the question is testing you on. With enough practice, you will recognize the same patterns over and over again and, by the end of your LSAT journey, you will achieve your target score.

For example, after doing about 200 logical-reasoning questions I knew exactly what the right answer should be and exactly what the wrong answers were going to be. Not word by word, of course, but structurally. It was almost like I could predict what the next sentence would say. For instance, if the stimulus started with "Some scientists believe...." I knew to anticipate the author's rebuttal as soon as I saw a "but" or "however" following it, as this was the "hard break" foreshadowing the author's argument.

For me, the hardest part, however, was rewiring my brain to think logically. I did almost every Prep Test (1-77) and had trouble internalizing the core fundamentals—basic elements such as determining the difference between what must be true, could be true, and cannot be true. Another important factor I struggled with early on was understanding arguments (i.e., deciphering the conclusion and evidence in support of each one).

For example, in the beginning I would focus solely on identifying the keywords (*thus, since, for, however,* etc.) in an argument, for example, and try to race through the test without really understanding what the author is saying (i.e., without properly paraphrasing). No doubt relying on keywords is important and helpful, but not necessary. What is needed is to really understand the basics. Thus, after 480 hours of hard-core studying I figured out how to rewire my brain with the fundamentals.

As a result, I decided to write this book. The goal of this book is to help you really understand how to think like the test-makers want you to think, and the purpose is for it to be used *before* you take a prep course or hire a tutor (or both). What you won't find in this book are actual test questions, as you will see hundreds of those during your practice. Rather, it will be pure raw strategy that provides you with best practices per question type and a method on how to think (with thinking scripts).

If you come from a marketing or sales background or haven't studied philosophy, political science, or logic before, then this book is for you. My goal is to get you to an LSAT score of 150 or close to it, as that is necessary to hit a perfect score of 180; in other words, without a 150 you can never get a 180. More importantly, it's at this benchmark that you will not only get into law school, but get merit scholarships or tuition discounts (assuming your GPA is sufficient).

The law-school business model works by requiring the people who get into law school with no scholarship offers to pay the full sticker price of the tuition bill. A portion of this then goes to fund and attract the high LSAT scorers so their tuition bill is fully or substantially complimentary, or "comped." The higher the incoming LSAT scores for the school, the better ranking they get in *U.S. News and World Report*, which in turn attracts more applicants to apply. Therefore it's critical to break 150 on the LSAT. If you are already scoring a 150 or more in your practice tests, then this book won't necessarily exclude you, but rather serve as a refresher for you as you aim to reach your personal target score.

Whereas most LSAT books focus on dumping information and expecting you to just understand it, from the top down, you'll learn how to internalize the material from the

INTRODUCTION: RELEARNING HOW TO THINK

bottom up from my perspective—that of a student who had a challenging time learning how to rethink. Furthermore, you will find the most value by revisiting this brief but powerful manual once a week (on a Sunday, for example). Think of it as music. When you hear your favorite song it takes you back to the time when you first heard it. It's nostalgia.

Similarly, when you get flustered on an LSAT problem or concept, I want your mind to think back to the very essential elements found in this book. This is my second goal with this book. Revisit it once a week and by the time you take the actual LSAT, each question should trigger a fundamental element found in this book to help you conquer the test.

I kept the concepts in this book down to the basics—simple and easy to understand. I also kept it short and to the point. I'm not going to talk about "what the LSAT is" and "what to do on test day"; you can read that at www.lsac.org. What I will do is give you my thought process regarding what led me to beat the LSAT relative to my starting point. For example, because I was never taught how to think critically, I forced myself to answer certain mental questions every time I did a problem. Thus, you will find all my thinking scripts in this book.

Sure, I didn't score in the 99th percentile, but just because the author of another LSAT book did score in the 99th percentile, it doesn't mean you will too. (That's the part-to-whole logical fallacy—stay tuned.) Besides, most "intelligent" 99th-percentile test-takers tend to author guides with statements like "think critically" or "think about the 'what ifs,'" or "disagree with the author" or "see if the evidence is relevant to the conclusion," but rarely give you a step-by-step scripted thought process on knowing how to do so. But as a student I'm thinking, *what does that mean, exactly? Hold my hand; I need that.*

That's like giving a 16-year-old, who has never driven before, a set of keys to your stick-shift Porsche and saying, "Okay, pick me at the airport in 45 minutes." How? They need to know how to open up the door, where to put the key, how to adjust the mirrors, how to reverse, how to put the car in the proper gears, how to turn, how to brake, etc. If they have no instructions they will likely crash, just as you would if you took the LSAT with no training or practice.

That is where this book comes in. It will give you realistic, results-oriented thinking methods that can help you gain points where you need them the most. I'm not saying not to take a test-prep course or have a brilliant, 99th-percentile teacher show you the ropes. What I am saying is that, for those who need more of a fundamental how-to thinking book from a non-99th-percentile scorer, this book will necessarily provide tremendous value. In other words, if you are scoring under 150 naturally and want to see a boost in your score, then it makes sense to learn from someone who naturally thinks like you, and who has gained at least 15 points on the LSAT.

The biggest thing to remember is that this is a skill that can be learned. If I told you that you would be starting on a basketball team in 90 days and you never played before at all, you would first need to learn how to dribble a ball, run up and down the court, practice shooting at the rim from the

INTRODUCTION: RELEARNING HOW TO THINK

free-throw line, and put hours of time in to perfect your skill. So, in 90 days, those skills would come naturally to you. It's the same with prepping for and taking the LSAT.

I proved this by taking two weeks off after sitting for my October 2015 test. After coming out of the test I decided that I needed a break to avoid mental exhaustion. So, I did anything but the LSAT. The minute I got back into studying, I noticed a big shift in accuracy and timing. I was rusty. *What do I do again for a strengthen question? That's right: negate by adding a "not" in front of a potential overlooked weakened possibility.* (Right?) Although I didn't forget the strategy, it took a while to remember it and, most importantly, to not pick the wrong answer choice.

It's like learning a foreign language. If you stop practicing it, you'll notice it fade away. This is no different. You have to master the strategies, and do it daily so it's second nature. If someone woke you up at 3 a.m., dragged you out of bed, moved you to the kitchen counter, turned on the halogen lights, gave you a pencil and a prep test, and said "Ready? Go!" could you answer questions correctly within the time limit? If you cannot answer yes to this question a week before your scheduled test, then don't take it; a "yes" response is necessary.

Here is the truth about the LSAT. It's learnable, but not all people start at the same level. If you are gifted, brilliant, a natural test-taker, have an amazing memory, etc. (i.e., score above a 160 naturally), then maybe this book isn't for you. However, if your dream is to become a lawyer, you are willing to put in the long hours, and really want to improve your score, then you will get a lot of value from this text. Unfortunately, I had no philosophy or political-science background, and didn't go to private school, so the first time I had ever seen a logic problem in my 30-plus years of life was a couple of months ago.

Whether my environment growing up or natural ability caused my current vantage point didn't matter. I saw results. If you put in the hours of learning the material and practice, you too will see results. The real question is "How badly do you want it?" Being a business major is a gift and a curse. It's a gift because I think naturally about business. I'm always thinking in terms of profit and loss statements.

If I'm having coffee I automatically think about how many tickets the establishment is doing, what their cup of coffee must cost, what they pay each employee, what their price per square foot is on the lease, how many sales they need to break even, what their profit margins are, where their biggest competitor is located, etc. I'm looking at the sales pitch that the employees are giving the customers. Are they upselling them to have a pastry in addition to the coffee? What's the wait time? Is the staff friendly or rude? This is how my mind thinks.

It's also a curse because if someone makes an argument, I'm not thinking about if his or her conclusion necessarily follows or probably follows. This is what I had to learn 30-plus years later, after a lifetime of no logical-reasoning training or experience. This is what you also will learn now and take with you in your careers. Mastering all sections of the LSAT is a beautiful skill that you will develop. It will enable you to rip through arguments, strengthen and weaken claims, point out flaws, and deduce the truth. Your mind will become a razor and your words will become your weapon. No guns needed.

This was the missing element in my life, the "self-actualization phase" in Maslow's hierarchy of needs that I traded off for a comfortable but complacent lifestyle. Being a lawyer is not about the money. Look around you: there is a lawyer on every corner, just as there is a dentist, a real-estate broker, an accountant, a barber, etc. It's about the power of language and what you can do with it to make a difference. So, if you really want it and are willing to put in the hard work, let's get started. It's an exciting journey.

2

LSAT: READY, STEADY, GO

To excel on the LSAT, and in law school, you need to learn and master four major skills: making deductions; understanding formal logic; determining if conclusions in an argument are necessary, probably follow, or don't follow from the evidence; and reading for main point and structure (not facts). Each question on the LSAT will test you from these four main brackets. However, underlying the four major skills are three necessary building blocks that must be mastered prior: finding the truth, understanding sufficiency versus necessity, and cause-and-effect thinking.

Finding the Truth (0-100)
First comes finding the truth. Although the test is multiple choice and naïvely perceived as "easy" by some, each answer

choice will seem, in some way, to fit perfectly as the "right answer," making the test challenging within the time constraints. Maybe one word will be different, such as *most* versus *some* or *could* versus *will*; that can have you contemplating the correct answer choice for minutes. Also, the actual question being asked can be just as tricky. For example: "Which one of the following could be true except...?" or "Which one of the following could be false except...?" So, to start, you need to understand what these tricky words all mean. An easy way to do so is put simple numbers behind them from 0-100:

1. All = 100
2. Most = 50-100
3. Some are not ("not all") = 0-99
4. Most are not = 0-49
5. Some = 1-100
6. None = 0

First, when someone says "all," they are referring to everyone in that class. If all smart people drink coffee, then 100 percent of people who are smart drink coffee. It's considered a "universal statement," as it refers to everyone in that universe of smart people. Universal statements are also called "categorical statements" and are very precise as they affirm or deny something about an entire category (either all or none). An example of saying that someone is not in a class is a "none" or "0" statement.

Next, if it's not a universal statement (all or none), it's a particular statement that refers to a portion of a class (*few, some, most*). "Most" is the majority, so think 50-100. The word "some" means that at least one person who's smart drinks coffee. So this means 1-100, and can include all but doesn't have to. Next is "not all" or "some are not," which mean the same thing: 0-99. If not all people who are smart drink coffee, then it's excluding everyone in that class. The same goes with "most are not," which means that the majority of smart people don't drink coffee (0-49).

Each LSAT question and answer choice use one of these tricky words. If you understand them with numbers on a scale from 0-100, it will help you visualize exactly what the question is asking you for. Another way of analyzing these words is with the following terms:

1. Must Be True ("MBT") = 100
2. Could Be True ("CBT") = 1-100
3. Could Be False ("CBF") = 0-99
4. Must Be False ("MBF") = 0

If a question asks, "Which one of the following must be true?" it is asking you about 100 percent of the time—no exceptions. Thus, what Could Be True and Must Be False are wrong. Although "Could Be True, 1-100" may include 100, it doesn't all of the time, so it's a wrong answer. It's the same with "Must Be False." You need to find an answer that is false (0) every single time. Here you will be looking for an answer choice that contradicts the premise or rule every single time. If it Could Be False (0-99), or Must Be True (100), both answers are wrong. In terms of real life, there are three main categories of finding the truth:

1. True (MBT) = 100
2. Possible (CBT/CBF) = 1-100; 0-99
3. False (MBF) = 0

What is not true (100) is merely possible (1-100) or false (0). Lots of times, the question may ask you, "Which one of the following must be true except . . . ?" and this is what the answer choice is asking you to find. Conversely, if it's not false (0), then it's merely possible (1-100) or true (100). Again, "Which one of the following must be false except . . . ?" is asking you for 1-100 (possible or true) as the correct answer choice.

Finally, if the question is asking you for "Could Be True," it's asking you to find something that has a 1-100 chance of happening. If it's asking you for "Could Be False," it has a 0-99 chance of happening. With the word "except" thrown into the question, you're looking for the logical opposite. The logical opposite of "Could Be True" is "Must Be False" (0). Likewise, the opposite of "Could Be False" is "Must Be True" (100). Here is a summary chart to analyze what you are being asked to find:

Logical Opposite Scales
1. True (100) . . . . Not True (99-0)
2. False (0) . . . . .Not False (1-100)
3. Could Be True (1-100). . . . . . . Must Be False (0)
4. Could Be False (0-99) . . . . . Must Be True (100)

The key is not to confuse a logical opposite with a polar opposite. For example, "true" and "not true" are logical opposites, whereas "true" and "false" are polar opposites (i.e., they are on the other end of the spectrum from 0 to 100). The majority of points have been lost simply by not understanding what to look for. Test-makers are really savvy and want to make sure you understand how to find the truth on test day, in law school, and in real life when you're going "to bat" for your client. Don't worry: once you get enough practice under your belt, you will be able to find the truth and go 0 to 100 real quick on the LSAT.

Sufficiency vs. Necessity
The second core building block involves knowing the difference between what is sufficient and what is necessary. Something that is "sufficient" is enough to guarantee a result. The result is "necessary" and depends on the sufficient event. For example, in a hypothetical world, if I drive my Lamborghini (sufficient event) then I'll get to work on time (necessary event). Getting to work on time depends on me driving my Lamborghini in this world. If I didn't get to

work on time, that means I did not drive my Lamborghini.

The most important takeaway is to know that the sufficient condition (driving my "Lambo") is not needed (i.e., the only thing) to get to work on time; it's not necessary. However, it definitely is a very powerful way (i.e., stronger than what's just needed) and enough, in and of itself, to guarantee that I won't be late. There still could be tons of other powerful (sufficient) ways in which I could get to work on time (bus, train, jet, helicopter, etc.). Test-makers love to put the sufficient condition as a necessary condition to trip you up. They will say, "Oh well, you didn't drive your Lambo (assuming it's needed and there is no other way), so you didn't get to work on time." No; again, there are tons of ways I could get to work on time. Driving my Lambo is not the only way (see Appendix I). Let's break this down:

If-Then Conditional Statement:

↳ If I drive my Lambo, then I will get to work on time.

Mistaking Sufficient for Necessary, a.k.a. Mistaken Negation:

↳ If I did not drive my Lambo, then I did not get to work on time.

When figuring out what is sufficient and what is necessary simply ask, "Okay, which term is needed by or dependent upon the other?" That is the necessary term. Then ask which term is enough to guarantee something else to happen. That is the sufficient term. The difference between sufficient and necessary is a heavily tested concept in the logic-games section, as well as the logical-reasoning question types, such as assumption and inference questions.

Many "sufficient assumption" questions will ask you to identify the "powerful" assumption (i.e., the unstated premise) that is enough to guarantee the conclusion in the argument. Likewise, many "necessary assumption" questions will ask you to identify which assumption is necessary to the argument. (Without it, the argument falls apart.) This difference is a very easy concept, something we use in daily life all the time. It's also known as a conditional or *if-then* statement. If I do this, then something else will happen.

The easiest way for me to internalize this concept was with a simple example about drinking my favorite energy drink: Red Bull. So, let's say one day I forget to dig into my bulk-purchased box from Costco and leave the house without it. I stop at the nearest gas station and walk into the convenience store.

I see a sign that says "$6.00 for a 24 oz. Red Bull." Let's say I only have $3.00. Would that be necessary or sufficient? Necessary. I must have at least $3.00 to purchase it; without $3.00 I cannot purchase it. Now, let's say that I reach into my pocket and find a $100 bill (big face, of course). Would that be necessary or sufficient? Well, it's not necessary because I only need $6.00 or less. So, it would be sufficient. It's more than enough to guarantee that I can buy my favorite drink—Red Bull.

Now, let's say I have exactly $6.00. Would that be sufficient or necessary? Both. It's enough to guarantee the purchase and it's needed. How about I go to the cashier, take my shirt off, and give it to her, in lieu of cash for the Red Bull? Would that be sufficient or necessary? Neither. Although she might be tempted, it would be irrelevant or "out of scope," just like many wrong answers that may tempt you on the LSAT.

Now, sticking with the gas-station reference, let's say the cashier says to me, "No shirt, no service." What would be necessary and what would be sufficient? Okay, first ask what is needed or depends upon the other. Well, getting "no service" depends on my "not wearing a shirt," so that is necessary. Likewise, "not wearing a shirt" is enough to guarantee my not getting service, so that is the sufficient part.

If-Then Conditional Statement:

➥ If no shirt, then no service.

Regardless of whether the "if-then" is included, the statement is still conditional. One event depends upon another event. Now, if the argument concludes, "If I didn't get service, then I didn't have a shirt on," that is a flaw known as a mistaken reversal; it takes something that was simply needed (getting no service) as a sufficient event and reverses it so it guarantees something else to happen (not having a shirt on). It's backwards, reversed. In any conditional argument, the necessary part doesn't guarantee something else.

Mistaken Reversal, a.k.a. Mistaking Necessary for Sufficient:

↳ If no service, then no shirt.

All this also can be put into a common "if-then" statement. The words after the "if" are sufficient and the words after the "then" are necessary. Note: "if-then" statements only apply to universal or categorical "all" statements, not particular statements with words such as "some" or "most." This is because you are saying that if X happens, then Y necessarily follows: no question, no doubts. It must be true for everyone in the group. It is the truth. If you say if X happens then Y "could" happen, then you're giving an "out" or being vague, and now it's not a Must Be True (100%) result, but rather a Could Be True (1-100%) result. In this case, the conclusion doesn't necessarily follow.

↳ If no shirt, then no service.

Another way of looking at this "if-then" statement is to say that if someone receives service, they are wearing a shirt. This is the logical equivalent and must be true at all times. This is known as the "contrapositive." You reverse the sufficient and necessary terms and take away a "not," or put a negative in front of the terms (i.e., add a "not") if the original statement is affirmative. Here again, the contrapositive only applies to universal statements (all, none) and not particular statements (some, most), since it's a rule that applies to everyone, not just a few.

- If service, then shirt on. (Contrapositive)

In summary, the two main traps, or logical flaws, on the LSAT are negating the terms without reversing them (mistaken negation) and just reversing the terms without negating them (mistaken reversal). Here's another breakdown of these important terms:

Valid Statements (MBT)

- If no shirt on, then no service. (If-Then Statement)
- If service, then shirt on. (Contrapositive)

Logical Flaws (CBT/CBF)

- If shirt on, then service. (Mistaken Negation)
- If no service, then no shirt on. (Mistaken Reversal)

Although these logical flaws could be true, they also could be false (you don't know) and thus are not necessarily true, like the contrapositive and the original if-then statement. This is the definition of validity. For something to be valid, it must be true. If it's not Must Be True (i.e., it's a Could Be False, or Must Be False), then the argument is not valid.

In real life, however, things are rarely 100 percent true or false. They are usually just possible. The trick lies in making something possibly lean more toward "more likely" (i.e., CBT) or toward "less likely" (CBF). This is what being a lawyer is all about: arguing your way to greater likelihood for your clients so you can get that win for them. Now you know why so many LSAT logical-reasoning problems ask you to strengthen or weaken the argument.

The test-makers love testing these mistakes of sufficient vs. necessary in the logical-reasoning section, and will often switch up what is sufficient and what is necessary to see if you really understand what is needed and what is simply enough to require the other part from happening in a relationship. Thus, always ask yourself, "What is needed in this relationship?" and "Without this part, can the other part still work?" If the answer to this second question is "no," you found the necessary part. The LSAT is all about relationships. They will give you two (or more) ideas/concepts and require you to analyze them backwards and forwards.

To help better understand sufficient and necessary relationships, you need to be able to identify keywords, or logical indicators. Some terms in a sentence that indicate sufficiency include: *if, when, where, whenever, whatever, every, all, any, anyone, no, none, the only,* and *people who.* Here you are referring to everyone in the class, not a portion of the class. Some terms that refer to the necessary side of the conditional statement are: *only, only if, only when, only where, requires, always, then, must, unless, until, without, depends upon, needs,* and *only where.* Anything after the sufficiency words is the powerful guarantee for something else to happen, while anything after the necessary words is the result that happens, which depends upon the sufficient part.

So, if you see "If xyz," the "xyz" is sufficient. Likewise, if you see "Only if abc," then the "abc" is the necessary part that depends upon the "xyz." Once you do enough practice with "if-then" statements, you will become extremely sensitive to them. You will notice them everywhere. Thus, you will master the secret language of lawyers (see Appendix A). One good indicator of knowing whether you have mastered these statements is to read a statement with no "if-then" keywords and know if it's a conditional statement or not. For example, if I say, "I won't drink anything that is carbonated," what's sufficient and what's necessary?

The sufficient term is "carbonated" and the necessary term is "not drinking." So this example translates to "If carbonated, then not drinking." Even without the keywords, you know that if any drink is carbonated that is guaranteed to ensure you won't drink it. What's interesting about sufficient and necessary conditions is that they can be matched with any corresponding keywords and still mean the same thing. This was a big "ah-ha" moment for me and another indicator that I finally internalized this concept.

1. Sufficient Keywords:
Every time something is carbonated . . .
All carbonated drinks . . .
Whenever something is carbonated . . .
Each time something is carbonated . . .
If something is carbonated . . .

2. Necessary Keywords:
. . . . **then** I won't drink
. . . . **must** be that I'm not drinking
. . . . **requires** that I can't drink
. . . . **depends** upon my not drinking
. . . . **only if** I'm not drinking.

Now what happens if the sufficient condition talks about more than one idea? For example, if I drive my Lambo or drink a Red Bull, then I will fly. Notice that the sufficient condition now has an "or" in it. This is saying that either item (driving a Lambo *or* drinking a Red Bull) is enough to guarantee that I will fly (the necessary condition). So, if I do one and not the other, I'm flying. This means that if I do both, I will fly as well. In the LSAT the "or," by default, is inclusive, unless stated otherwise. Conversely, if either the argument section or the logic games (which test this concepts heavily) says "but not both," then either sufficient condition (driving in my Lambo *or* drinking a Red Bull) will guarantee the result (flying), but it cannot be both.

To take the contrapositive of this is simple. You reverse and negate, as usual, but this time you change the "or" to an "and." This is a rule that you must memorize for test day. So the contrapositive would be:

**Valid Statements (MBT)—"OR"
in Sufficient Conditions**

↳ If drive my Lambo *or* drink a Red Bull, then I will fly.
   (IF-THEN STATEMENT)

↳ If I didn't fly, then I didn't drive my Lambo *and* didn't drink a Red Bull. **(CONTRAPOSITIVE)**

Next, if you have an "and" in the sufficient condition, then both ideas (not just one) in your hypothetical world must happen to trigger the result from happening. Note: they are not "either or"; both must happen. Again, with the contrapositive do the same thing: reverse, negate, and change the "and" back to an "or."

**Valid Statements (MBT)—"AND"
in the Sufficient Condition**

↳ If drive my Lambo *and* drink a Red Bull, then I will fly.
   (IF-THEN STATEMENT)

↳ If I didn't fly, then I didn't drive my Lambo *or* drink a Red Bull. **(CONTRAPOSITIVE)**

Okay: how about if the "or" or "and" is in the necessary condition? For example: if I drive my Lambo, then I'll either get to work on time **or** get a ticket. This is saying that one event is enough to guarantee two possible results (or both, unless stated otherwise). Alternatively, let's look at this example: if I drive my Lambo, then I'll get to work on time **and** get a ticket. This is guaranteeing two possible results that Must Be True. When you see an "and" in the necessary condition, it's like a kind of grammar shortcut. Instead of writing the sentence over again with the second clause, you just merge them together with the conjunction "and." In other words, it's saying that both results must happen. To contrapose the statements you follow the same method: reverse, negate, replace all instances of "and" with "or" or vice versa:

Valid Statements (MBT)—"OR" in the Necessary Condition

- If drive my Lambo, then I'll get to work on time *or* get a ticket. **(IF-THEN STATEMENT)**

- If I didn't get to work on time *and* didn't get a ticket, then I didn't drive my Lambo. **(CONTRAPOSITIVE)**

Valid Statements (MBT) —"AND" in the Necessary Condition

- If drive my Lambo, then I'll get to work on time *and* get a ticket. **(IF-THEN STATEMENT)**

- If I didn't get to work on time *or* didn't get a ticket, then I didn't drive my Lambo. **(CONTRAPOSITIVE)**

Finally, how about if the "or" or "and" is in both the sufficient and the necessary conditions? You still perform the same tasks: reverse, negate, change all "and's" to "or's" or "or's" to "and's." For example, if I drive my Lambo **or** get a ticket, then I'll get to work on time **and** speed. What's the contrapositive?

Valid Statements (MBT) —"OR" in the Sufficient Condition, "AND" in the Necessary Condition

- If drive my Lambo *or* get a ticket, then I'll get to work on time *and* speed. **(IF-THEN STATEMENT)**

- If I didn't get to work on time *or* didn't speed, then I didn't drive in my Lambo *and* didn't get a ticket. **(CONTRAPOSITIVE)**

Valid Statements (MBT) —"AND" in the Sufficient Condition, "OR" in the Necessary Condition

- If drive my Lambo *and* get a ticket, then I'll get to work on time *or* speed. **(IF-THEN STATEMENT)**

- If I didn't get to work on time *and* didn't speed, then I didn't drive in my Lambo *or* didn't get a ticket. **(CONTRAPOSITIVE)**

No matter how bizarre or stupid the argument may sound, you must accept it to be true in the LSAT world. Hypothetical statements are not saying that something is necessarily true; it is saying that *if* it is true then something else happens. In other words, if you don't trigger the sufficient condition (i.e., don't press that button) then the hypothetical world disappears and any possibility could happen, not just the necessary portion. Also, if you just do the necessary condition on its own (the right side of the arrow) without doing the sufficient condition, then the if-then rule or hypothetical world also disappears since you didn't trigger the left side of the arrow (the sufficient condition).

So in basic, abstract form, if you don't do X (i.e., don't trigger the sufficient condition), then this rule doesn't apply. Also, if you just do Y (i.e., avoid the sufficient condition) on its own, then this rule is not triggered (this world doesn't exist); you're not hammering the "if X" button to initiate it to produce a result. You are completely avoiding it.

- If X, then Y. (If-Then Statement)
- If not Y, then not X. (Contrapositive)

Therefore, with any "if-then" rules you will have a couple of possibilities. In logic games, you would try to create multiple sketches to incorporate these scenarios because the questions will ask you about them anyway. So, the first one is when the rule or the contrapositive gets triggered. If you press the "if X" button then it will shoot off and do "Y." This is one outcome/sketch and must happen. Next, if you trigger the contrapositive sufficient condition "if not Y," then it will shoot off and do "not X," which is logically equivalent to the first statement and must happen.

Finally, the third possibility is if you just do the necessary conditions alone (i.e., you just do Y and not X) and avoid sufficient-condition buttons altogether. If a question, for example, asks you if "not X" happens, then it avoids the rule and it does not trigger sufficient conditions. As you will see later in logical-reasoning inference questions, the stimulus will give you "what if" scenarios and then give answer choices that simply "Could Be True" instead of "Must Be True." In this particular example, any answer choice that talks about not triggering the sufficient condition, or "if not X," is a Could Be True/False and is wrong, as inference questions require Must Be True answers.

In simple terms, once you have a condition (e.g., "if X, then Y"), if the trigger is pushed anything to the right of it (in this case, Y) must happen. Anything to the left of it simply could happen and is not a Must Be True, but rather a Could Be True answer. When in doubt, always remember inferences (MBT) go from left to right not right to left; never deduce by going against your right arrow.

MBT (Left to Right):

CBT (Right to Left):

←

Finally, the last important logical indicator(s) to master within the sufficient and necessary bracket is "unless/until/ without." Whenever you see these words you have to do two things. Identify the necessary condition of the sentence (i.e., the clause following unless/until/without) and, more importantly, negate the sufficient condition.

For example, take this statement: "I will cruise in my Lambo, unless it's raining outside." Here the necessary condition is it raining outside (as it follows after the word "unless") and the sufficient condition is cruising in my Lambo. To translate this into formal logic, you have to negate the sufficient condition so the proper if-then statement looks like this:

- I will cruise in my Lambo, unless it's raining outside. (original "unless" statement)

- If I don't cruise in my Lambo, then it's raining outside. (correct translation; negates the sufficient condition)

- If it's not raining outside, then I will cruise in my Lambo. (correct contrapositive)

The best strategy for the LSAT is to commit these rules to memory and practice daily in your LSAT prep book. Mastering the LSAT is a skill and if you don't practice a skill you will get rusty, just like with learning a foreign language; stay on top of your game by practicing formal logic drills at least once a week. Many questions across all sections of the test (even reading comprehension) will be testing your ability to properly understand the sufficient versus necessary building blocks.

Cause and Effect: "The Married Couple"

Unlike if-then universal statements, which fit into "all or none" scenarios, a cause-and-effect relationship isn't necessarily true in all cases; it's used in particular cases. In a cause-and-effect relationship one event is the reason why (i.e., the cause) the other event happens (i.e., the effect). One event is making the other event occur and therefore must occur before the effect occurs (unlike with sufficient and necessary relationships). The key is that the cause must come before the effect (in other words, chronology is necessary), as opposed to sufficient and necessary statements, which can happen at the same time (as long as they happen).

(Cause-and-Effect Statement)

- Studying for four hours a day can cause an increase in your score on the LSAT.

Here, studying for four hours a day is the possible reason for (cause) for an increase in your LSAT score (the effect). However, notice how it doesn't apply all the time, as it does in an if-then conditional statement. Someone can study for four hours a day for one section of the test but fail the next three sections of the test, resulting in an overall decrease in one's score. It's possible in some circumstances, but not every circumstance. In many cause-and-effect statements you will also find what I call "hedging words" that do not guarantee the result and easily could be weakened or strengthened in the logical-reasoning section (such as *may*, *could*, or *can*).

The great thing about the cause-and-effect relationship is that the test-makers make the assumption that the "cause" indicated (e.g., studying for four hours) is the only possible reason for the effect (e.g., to see an increase in your LSAT score). This holds up when the cause-and-effect relationship is in the conclusion of the argument. This is why I call this relationship the married couple as they always go together.

"The Home-Wrecker"
Now, what's one way to wreck a marriage? Introduce a home wrecker. You can think of tons of other possibilities to increase your LSAT score. For example, alternative causes could include studying only three hours a day, or eight hours a day, or not studying at all. Maybe taking a magic pill (like in the movie *Limitless*), along with four hours of studying, caused an increase in your score. Also, maybe the two events are simply just a coincidence and there is no cause-and-effect relationship at all. Since the cause must come before the effect, a great way to weaken a causal argument is to show that the effect happened (an increase in your LSAT score) without the cause happening (studying for four hours). Alternatively, you could show that the cause happened, but the effect just didn't happen (you studied for four hours but your LSAT score decreased).

Conversely, to strengthen the argument, pick an answer that removes one of these alternative possibilities. An example would be "Studying for less than four hours a day doesn't increase your LSAT score." Notice how, by turning this possibility into a negative (i.e., adding a "not" word, such as "didn't"), you eliminated that possibility.

Another way to strengthen the argument is to focus in on activating the cause to make the effect happen; find something that triggers the cause to push the effect out. For example, let's say that the library is only open from 12 p.m. to 4 p.m. and you're only allowed to park your car there for four hours and 15 minutes; otherwise, it will get towed. This will make sure that when you get to the library at 12 p.m., you are doing your four hours and getting out: nothing more, nothing less. Once your cause (four hours of studying) is activated, then you will see an increase in your score. Since the cause must come before the effect, you know that will ensure that the effect happens.

Also, when looking at a cause-and-effect relationship, it's important to see if the cause-and-effect statement is in the premises or the conclusion. Premises always have to be accepted as true on the LSAT, so it may or may not be flawed. However, if it's in the conclusion, automatically think about other possible causes to weaken the argument or to point out the flaw. To strengthen the argument, eliminate the same possibilities (with a "not") and focus on activating the married couple (i.e., the cause-and-effect duo).

Many LSAT arguments will have a coincidence or correlation (two events happening together at one time or several times) in the evidence and then conclude that the one event caused the second event. Here's an example: P correlates with Q; therefore P causes Q. This correlation/causation pattern is tested frequently on the LSAT and to strengthen or weaken it, do as follows:

Pattern One:
Evidence: P correlates with Q
Conclusion: so P causes Q

- To weaken (3 ways):
  - Q causes P (reverse happens)
  - R causes P and Q (something else happens)
  - Relationship is simply a coincidence (it's just random)

- To strengthen (add a "not" to a weakened possibility):
  - Rule out Q causing P (rule out reverse happening)
  - Rule out R causing P and Q (rule out something else happening)
  - Rule out relationship simply being a coincidence (say it's not random)
  - Also, add more evidence showing that P actually caused Q.

Pattern Two:
Evidence: P causes Q
Conclusion: Causation is true (author agrees)

- To weaken: (show problems with study/evidence)
  - P occurs and Q does not occur
  - P does not occur but Q does occur
  - an alternate cause is identified (includes reversal—Q causes P)

- To strengthen (add a "not" to weaken an alternative possibility; show no problems with study/evidence):
  - P occurs and Q occurs
  - P does not occur Q does not occur
  - Q does not cause P (reversal can't happen)
  - an alternate cause, "R," cannot be the case (alternative possibility can't happen)

Now that we've established these basic building blocks, let's move on to the sections of the test itself. First up: logical reasoning.

3

LOGICAL REASONING IS SELECTIVE REASONING

To master the logical-reasoning section of the LSAT (which makes up 50% of the test), you need to understand what the test-makers want from you. They want to know whether, based on the evidence given (studies, facts, scientific data, correlation, etc.), the conclusion (author's opinion) follows necessarily (100% of the time), sometimes (1-100% of the time) or not at all (0% of the time). In other words, whether the conclusion must be true, is merely possible, or cannot be true based on the evidence.

This concept, although it may seem simple, took me weeks of preparation to understand and is the reason why I call it "selective reasoning." The key to analyzing an argument is selecting the conclusion and evidence apart from the rest of the argument (i.e., the set-up) and examining them under a microscope to see how the conclusion follows from the evidence.

Don't Get Lost in the Sauce

The conclusion is nothing more than the main point of the author; what is he or she trying to convince you of? The evidence is the "why," or the support for the main point. What's the reasoning? What's the proof? Filler or background or contextual information is the "set-up" the author will present to give you an understanding of what the argument is about. Many times, the true intention is to get you "lost in the sauce." One way in which the test writers will increase difficulty is give you multiple arguments within the stimulus. They usually begin with statements such as "Some people believe..." or "Scientists claim..." and will give you some person's viewpoint with their supporting evidence; then you will find the author's rebuttal of that point, with his or her own viewpoint. Now you have two arguments to decipher in relation to one another. Let's take a closer look at this structure:

Common Argument Structures
1. Other viewpoint: "Some scientists believe..."
2. Evidence for other viewpoint: indicated by *since*, *because*, etc.
3. Author rebuttal following other person's viewpoint: indicated by *however*, *but*, *yet*, etc. (A "hard break" occurs, jumping to the author's argument.)
4. Author's conclusion: very opinionated words ending in "-ly," or a statement prescribing something ("we should not do

X; we should do Y; X is good or not good; I prefer X over Y; X does cause Y; X is less than Y," etc.)
5. Author's evidence, following keywords such as "for" or "given that," or a colon.

You may also find multiple background "set-ups" and sub-conclusions within main conclusions. When you think you have found the main point of an argument but then it keeps on going, what you found is really the sub-conclusion, which is now being used to further support the actual main point of the argument.

Another way in which deconstructing the conclusion apart from the evidence may be challenging is with heavy use of pronouns, vague clauses, and modifiers of verbs and nouns. The more "stacked" sentences become with adjectives and adverbs and pronouns, the more your eyes start glazing over and it's easy to get lost. So paying attention to specific keywords, skipping over certain sentences, and anticipating hard breaks in thoughts via the use of key words such as *but*, *yet*, and *however* is critical to breaking a 150 on the LSAT.

Overall, the anatomy of an argument is really simple. In fact, we make real-life arguments all the time. An argument is made up of a conclusion or opinion (You should do or not do X, something is good or not good, I agree or disagree with Y, something will or won't happen, etc.) backed up by support or evidence (facts, studies, etc.). However, in almost all arguments there is a gap between the conclusion and the support called the assumption, which is just an unstated piece of evidence.

Basic Argument Forms

Basic Argument Set-up:

E (stated evidence)

+

A (unstated evidence)

―――――――――――――

C (opinion)

Why is the assumption unstated? Maybe people just are lazy and don't have time to explicitly state it. Maybe they just expect you to understand it, as it may appear to be common knowledge. If you say "I like to go to the beach on a hot Sunday afternoon" without giving a reason for your assertion, then it's nothing more than just an opinion.

Basic Argument Set-up:

Evidence: none

+

Assumption: none

―――――――――――――

Conclusion: I like to go to beach on a hot Sunday afternoon.

I'm not going to do what you say just because you said it. That would be foolish. Nevertheless, every day people are moved to take some sort of action just because a famous person, doctor, politician, scientist, etc. said to do it. In fact, this "sales technique" is used all the time and is known as the "appeal to authority" logical fallacy (which we will cover later).

Now, the minute you say you want to go to the beach on hot Sunday afternoon because "you want to get a tan," you now have made an argument because you gave a reason, or a "why." This is now a subject to be attacked.

Basic Argument Set-up:

Evidence: I want to get a tan

+

Assumption: ?

___

Conclusion: I like to go to beach on a hot Sunday afternoon.

Are you assuming that on hot days you get tans? That only on hot Sunday afternoons you get tanned? Are you saying that every time you go to the beach on a hot Sunday afternoon you get a tan, so you will also next Sunday? Are you claiming that a hot Sunday afternoon causes you to get a tan? What if it doesn't? What if you go to the beach on a hot Sunday afternoon and don't get a tan? What if you get a tan just driving to the beach in the car and then go to the beach? As you can see now, your conclusion or opinion doesn't necessarily follow from the evidence 100% of the time. You see how there is a gap between your support and conclusion? This is what the LSAT requires you to uncover and attack.

If this were a simple LSAT argument that asked you to

weaken the argument, you can think of any other possibility to show that you went to the beach and didn't get a tan. Conversely, if you wanted to strengthen the argument, you could think of things that would show there is no other way to get a tan other than going to the beach on a hot Sunday afternoon (i.e., eliminate all the "what if" questions from the critics).

If the LSAT asked you to spot the assumption you would see how these two terms, "hot Sunday afternoon" and "tan," are linked and predict that they are related somehow. If this were a flaw question, you would see how the author overlooks various possibilities of getting tans by other methods other than just a the occasion of a hot Sunday afternoon. In other words, your job is to focus on the assumption. How you get questions wrong is by trying to negate the evidence or negate the conclusion without attacking the assumption. These are the biggest answer choice traps. You must figure out how to uncover the assumption and then attack it.

This is the beauty about studying for the LSAT. You learn how to think critically; you learn how to think like a lawyer. Before, when someone used to make a claim (e.g., a recommendation of some sort) I would listen and then agree or disagree: "Yeah, that makes sense," or "Yeah, that doesn't sound right." Now, after putting 480 hours into mastering LSAT material, I am automatically trained to ask for the evidence (the "why") and see if the conclusion follows necessarily or not. The minute someone gives me their reasoning, my mind is thinking about spotting the assumption pattern and thinking how to strengthen or weaken the claim, or figuring out how it's completely flawed. Thus, I argue that mastering LSAT study material makes you smarter.

The Olympic Long-Jumper

Every argument presented on the LSAT has an issue of some sort, since the conclusion doesn't follow from the evidence 100% of the time (i.e., it doesn't necessarily follow). Thus, your job is to strengthen, weaken, and find the assumption or flaw in it. This is very similar to what you will do as a lawyer. You will have evidence and make a claim to persuade a judge or jury. Your job is to show that your conclusion (guilty or not guilty) follows from the evidence, if not 100% of the time, then most of the time, or vice versa.

Thus, logic is all about finding the truth and separating it from the other possibilities. Remember: what could be true could also be false. When you start thinking about the "what if's" after you read or listen to the facts, "draw a line in the sand" and go read or listen to the conclusion. This is critical. You must not take in the entire stimulus or argument as if it were the last bite of a cookie.

The evidence and the conclusion must be separated in your mind. First, read the argument and say, "Okay, what is the conclusion saying?" Next, say, "It cannot be." I like to think of it as someone trying to scam me. My defenses are up and I'm very skeptical. Now I think of the exact opposite and think about other possibilities missing. Then ask, "What is the support or evidence for it?" Ask yourself if there a big hole in between. Does the arguer have to make a huge leap to get from one side of the sand (the evidence) to the other (the conclusion)? Is he or she an Olympic long jumper? Then, next to each question, put it into the basic argument form:

Basic Argument Form Completed:

E (stated evidence)—blah blah blah... "COULD HAPPEN"

+

A (unstated evidence): **could = will**
(e.g., pray on it, so it happens)

C (opinion)—yadda yadda yadda... "WILL HAPPEN"

A very simple example is when someone tells you that something *could* happen and then follows up by saying it *will* happen (above). Salespeople are notorious for this. "You could become a millionaire by following my wealth-building secrets by attending my apartment-flipping seminar this weekend (evidence), so after you attend you will learn everything you need to and become a millionaire (conclusion). There are only two seats remaining. Nearly sold out. Are you ready to become a millionaire?" Really? From "I could" to "I will"? This dude is definitely an Olympic long-jumper.

So now you see an example of how long the leaps can be from evidence to conclusion. How do you then know what must follow 100 percent of the time? This is called deductive reasoning using categorical arguments. Categorical evidence is what is true from an entire category or universe, is true of most of the people in it, or is true of some of the people in it.

For example, if you are in Ms. Hayek's class for the final and she gave everyone in the class an A, then guess what? You got an "A." This must be true 100% of the time. Assuming you were in the class, of course. But remember: on the LSAT the fact that you were in the class is a fact that is indisputable. You cannot deny that.

What you cannot do is say that since you were in the class (a fact) and you got an A, she probably gave everyone an A. Really? Three kids got a C. That just crushed your argument (your critic found a counterexample). Thus, you can never go from your particular circumstance and generalize to the entire category or universe.

However, note that in real life, because it's nearly impossible to study everyone in the world, science experiments study a large random sample size of particular cases (e.g., say 5000 people that have X always do Y) to see what patterns emerge to make a prediction that says something like "The next person that has X will do Y." Although the study is not representative of the entire world (all X people) the claim is that it's highly probable (likely) that Y will happen. In other words, it could be true, but it's not a Must Be True.

This type of "inductive reasoning," going from part to whole, depends heavily on having a random and sufficient sample size but is still not 100-percent bulletproof as deductive or categorical reasoning that talks about every single person or no people in a universe (all or none).

LOGICAL REASONING IS SELECTIVE REASONING

Many LSAT problems will throw statistics in the evidence to see if you catch whether or not the evidence is truly a representative, random, or not biased to generate a guaranteed conclusion (Must Be True) or merely a possible conclusion (Could Be True). If you were trying to weaken the argument above, what would you say? Well, you would want to show that when X happened, Y actually didn't, or that Y happened without X happening, or that Y happened first and then X happened, or maybe something else, like Z caused both X and Y to happen. Basically, you need to find possibilities to disprove (i.e., make it unlikely) that X will cause Y to happen.

Every time there is a study of some sort there's a data-input-and-output process that goes on. Data is gathered (input), it's processed, and it's churned out (output). A good study assumes that there are no biases from the input, and no skewed data during the processing to create a thorough output. Therefore, to strengthen the study, just find an answer choice that reflects this assumption (i.e., brings it to light), or to weaken, find the reverse, something that shows that the study was biased or the data was skewed.

Now that we have covered the basic argument form, let's get into what the second major task is to do in the logical reasoning section: finding the truth.

4

DEDUCING THE TRUTH IN INFERENCES

On the LSAT, in addition to criticizing arguments, your second main task for the logical-reasoning section is to find out or deduce simply what Must Be True, Could Be True, and Must Be False from two sets of facts (i.e., no argument). You will be given facts with categorical statements (all, every, if-then, none, no) and particular statements referring to just a part (some, many, few, most). By definition, if it's not referring to the entire category, then it's a particular statement—simple as that.

"All" Statements
When finding the truth, the rule is that what's true of the entire category (i.e., all of the category) is true of most of the category, and true of some of the category. Thus, you can go down in logic from "all to most to some," but not up from

"some to most to all" for a Must Be True (100%) conclusion. If you go up, the best you can say is Could Be True (1-100%), but you don't really know for certain, making the argument invalid. Remember: what could be true could also be false. Thus, the latter is making a generalization (like a stereotype) and is a logical flaw. The real world doesn't apply on the LSAT.

MBT vs. CBT

MUST BE TRUE 100% OF THE TIME (VALID)		COULD BE TRUE 1-100% OF THE TIME (INVALID)	
All		All	
Most	↓	Most	↑
Some		Some	

I'm a visual learner, so I internalized this concept by doing what I do best when I'm confused—sketching (although I make stick figures at best):

Every Student (S) in the class is getting an A grade (A).
Becky (B) is a Student in the class (S).
Therefore, Becky (B) is getting an A grade (A).

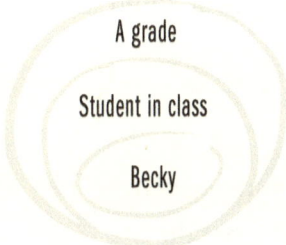

As you can see, Becky must receive an A grade. The same goes with categorical negative statements (*no, none* statements). No one in Ms. Hayek's class got an A on the final and if you were in the class that day, then guess what? You didn't get an A. This must be true 100% of the time.

MBF vs. CBF

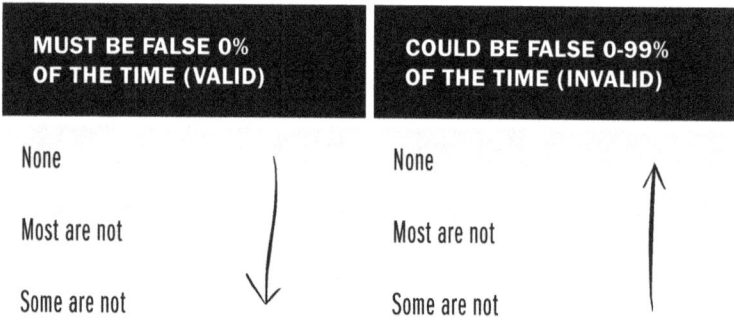

This means that if none got an A, then most students did not get an A and some students did not get an A. This must necessarily follow from the evidence 100% of the time. On the other hand, what simply could be true is going up the chain. If *some* students didn't get an A, it could be true that most didn't get an A and possible that none got an A but, again, you don't know with 100% certainty, thereby making the argument invalid as you can't generalize. Also remember: since it could be true it could also be false; you simply don't know.

"No" Statements

What's interesting about negative or "no" statements, and for me the hardest to get a handle on, is the mutual exclusivity of them. Unlike the affirmative categorical statements (*all*, *every*), where everyone fits nicely inside the circles, the negative statements show exclusivity. So, as you can see, if you were a student in the class, then you did not get an A.

You can also reverse a negative statement and analyze it from opposite sides since they are excluding each other. Anyone who got an A was not a student in the class (e.g., maybe they were an online student or in a different class).

Grades of Students in Class (possible B-F)

A Grade

Going down the logic chain is also known as making deductions, or making inferences, and is exactly what inference question types in logical reasoning want you to understand. Any inference question is going to ask you "What must be true?" or "What must be false?"

"Some" Statements
So what about particular (some or most) statements? Have you ever heard someone say, "Some people do X, so you should do it"? For example: "Kim Kardashian likes cats because they are low-maintenance animals as they go to the bathroom themselves, so you should get one."

Before studying for the LSAT I would have said, "Cool" or "Okay, I'll think about it," regardless of whether I liked cats or not. (I do have two cats, by the way.) I would agree or disagree with the statement instead of analyzing the statement. Now, when someone points out a particular case I automatically think of the other side:

"Great; guess what? William Shakespeare hated cats because they always wanted to sit on his lap and wouldn't leave him alone, so you shouldn't get one."

In other words, for every *some* that wants to do something there could be another some that doesn't. Therefore, whenever you see two some statements in an argument you cannot deduce a Must Be True conclusion, making it an invalid argument.

More importantly, to actually negate or disprove a particular, or *some*, statement you can show that no one does X (i.e., add a "not" to the sentence). If some equals 1-100, then the logical opposite of that is "none" or zero. Thus, if "some A's are B's," you can negate that by showing that "no A's are B's," or no one likes cats, so you shouldn't get one.

Another *some* statement can be "some cat lovers don't walk their cats," or some A's are not B's. The logical opposite of this particular negative statement is "all cat lovers walk their cats," or all A's are B's. If all is 100, the logical opposite is "not all" or 0-99, which is known as "some are not." So if all cat lovers walk their cats, then to negate that you can show some cat lovers don't walk their cats. Notice how you can analyze this from either side. "Some A's are not B's" (i.e., not necessarily all) and "all A's are B's" (necessarily all) are logical opposites. They cannot be both true (or false) at the same time.

Now to not negate but rather simply weaken the claim (i.e., not disprove it 100%), just show another possibility. For example, if the claim is that some cat lovers don't walk their cats, you can show that some cat lovers do walk their cats; if some don't, it could be possible that some do. So, now every time someone tells me "some X don't do Y," I instantly respond by saying "some X does Y" to weaken their argument or find proof that all X does Y, in order to destroy their argument. This was my favorite "a-ha" moment (my internal deduction) when studying the LSAT. This is awesome. Here is how it looks visually:

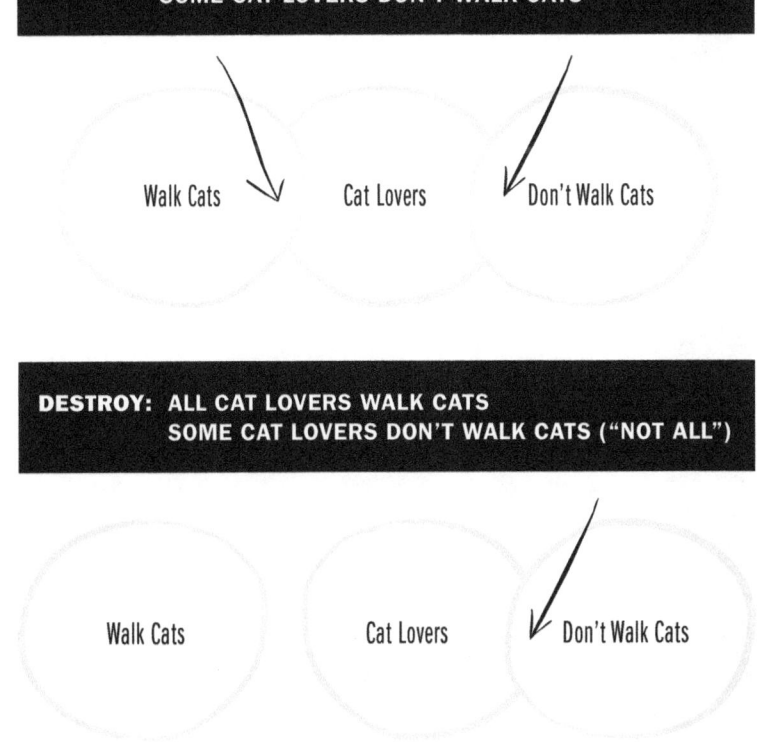

Thus, every time you read a set of facts you must think of its categorical structure. This includes whether each premise is talking about the entire universe or just a part. Also, whether the premise is affirmative or negative. Finally, think about logically destroying the fact by providing the logical opposite, as shown in the crisscross arrows below.

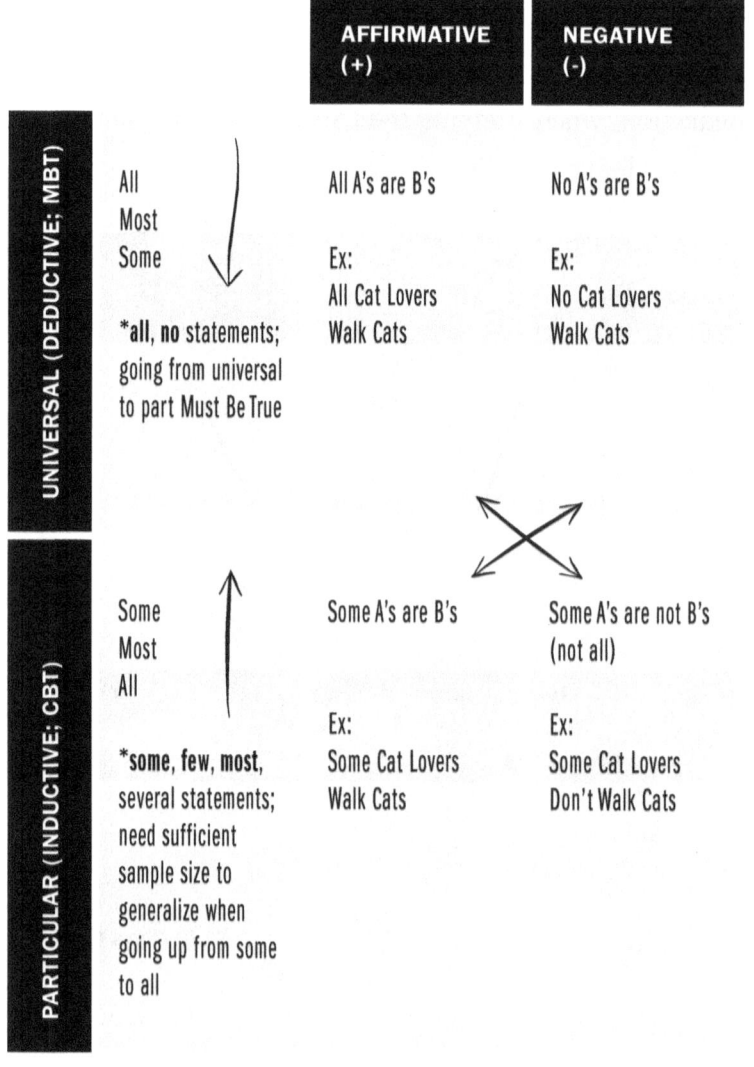

DEDUCING THE TRUTH IN INFERENCES

These are the critical-inference skills necessary for the logical-reasoning non-argument questions and the analytical reasoning, or logic games, section of the LSAT. Next, let's jump into the bread and butter of arguments: assumptions.

5

CLOSING THE GAP: FINDING THE ASSUMPTION

The biggest task and critical component of logical-reasoning arguments is uncovering the assumption. This is precisely what you need to attack and will be heavily tested on. In fact, the wrong-answer traps will be attacking the evidence or attacking the conclusion without addressing the gap in between the two. So, how does a conclusion then not necessarily follow from the evidence? How can you spot the "Olympic jump" gap? There are two major ways.

Non-Related Arguments
The first way is when the evidence and conclusion are talking about two different things (i.e., they are not related). You start reading evidence about how, for example, a Rolex is a

luxury brand and then, all of a sudden, the author concludes with "Therefore, Rolex is profitable." You have "luxury brand" in the evidence and "profit" in the conclusion. If you read and say, "Where did the profit come from?" you have spotted two terms that are not relevant and have thus found how they don't necessarily follow. Here is a sample of a basic argument form with unrelated terms. How can you make the terms "relevant" and "tighten up" the argument?

Basic Argument Form:

Evidence: Rolex is a luxury brand.

+

Assumption? (i.e., unstated evidence)

Conclusion: Rolex is profitable.

So what can you do to tighten up the argument? How can you make the Olympic long jumper work smarter, not harder? How can you make the evidence click with the conclusion and make it necessarily (or more likely) to follow? You need to find the assumption (missing sentence or fact) that links the two terms to make sense. This is what the answer choice on the LSAT will present you with—a missing piece of evidence involving both terms. An assumption is like cement: it makes both things stick together and very difficult to tear apart.

Every time you have evidence saying "X" and a conclusion saying "Y" (i.e., they are not related), look for an answer choice that glues them together. You can glue them together in several ways. One way is to make them equal to each other. For example, in the Rolex argument, the assumption was that luxury = profit. Anything that is a luxury brand will be profitable.

Basic Argument Form Completed:

Evidence: Rolex is a luxury brand.

+

Assumption? Luxury brand = profit

Conclusion: Rolex is profitable.

What if the argument was "Rolex is not considered a luxury brand anymore; therefore, it's profitable"? Here the evidence says "not X" (not luxury) and the conclusion says "therefore Y" (profitable). The assumption would be: not luxury = profit. Anything that is not luxurious is profitable. Here the assumption is that X and Y don't go together.

Basic Argument Form Completed:

Evidence: Rolex is not a luxury brand.

+

Assumption? Not luxury brand = profit

Conclusion: Rolex is profitable.

Wait—how does that make sense? Rolex is luxurious, right? It doesn't matter if you agree or disagree with the evidence. In the LSAT world the evidence is always true. If they say that Rolex is not a luxury brand, then it's not a luxury brand—period.

How about if the argument was "Rolex is not luxurious; therefore Rolex is not profitable"? Now the evidence is saying "not X," and the conclusion is claiming "therefore not Y." Here the assumption is that X (i.e., being luxurious) is needed or depends upon Y (i.e., being most profitable). Anything that is profitable requires it to be luxurious. In formal logic terms: if profitable, then luxurious; if not luxurious, then not profitable. Does this look familiar? Well, it's the contrapositive form, as mentioned in chapter two.

Basic Argument Form Completed:

Evidence: Rolex is not a luxury brand.
+
Assumption? If not luxury = not profitable
Contrapositive: If profitable, then luxury

Conclusion: Rolex is not profitable.

Finally, how about if the argument says "I purchased the only limited-edition Rolex Sky-Dweller watch, which is, of course, luxurious; therefore all Rolex Sky-Dweller watches are luxurious." Did you notice the particular statement in the evidence ("I") and the categorical statement in the conclusion ("all")? This assumption is saying that my particular limited-edition Rolex Sky-Dweller represents all Rolex Sky-Dweller watches. The assumption is that some X is representative of all X. This is exactly the assumption you need to find in the answer choices.

Basic Argument Form Completed:

Evidence: I purchased the only limited-edition Rolex Sky-Dweller luxurious watch.

+

Assumption? One watch represents all watches (flawed).

Conclusion: All Rolex Sky-Dweller watches are luxurious.

This is a classic part-to-whole generalization, like a stereotype. Although it could be true, it doesn't necessarily have to be true. Thus, this is a common flaw pattern that the LSAT tests you on over and over again. Notice that it was uncovered in the assumption. Your success on the logical-reasoning argument section depends upon your figuring out the assumption and is what is going to enable you to bag huge points on the LSAT.

It's also what you need to attack or negate when you're asked to weaken the argument, to highlight or support when you are asked to strengthen the argument, to identify when you are asked to spot the assumption, and to figure out which flawed pattern the assumption falls into when you're asked to identify the flaw (as with the case above).

CLOSING THE GAP: FINDING THE ASSUMPTION

If you think you're just going to read the evidence, then read the conclusion, then deny the conclusion and "Voila." You found your right answer—think again. You need to go "hard" when figuring out the assumption. Once you predict it, you then identify it, and strengthen, weaken, or match it to a flaw pattern; this is critical. It took me a very long time to figure this out and only through time and working through countless LSAT problems did I train my mind to think critically and spot the assumptions.

On the LSAT you have about one minute and 30 seconds to answer each logical reasoning question. Don't worry, though; speed comes with timing drills and timing drills come with mastering the material. Therefore _____. Can you make the deduction? What must necessarily follow from the sentence above? Speed implies mastery.

Premise 1: Speed → Timing
Premise 2: Timing → Mastery
Therefore . . .

---

1) Speed comes with Mastery (Must Be True).
2) Not Mastery, then Not Speed (Contrapositive—MBT).
(Mastery is dependent on speed.)

Don't worry if you didn't see this right a way. When I first started, it took me weeks to understand valid argument forms. After three months, I was spotting arguments everywhere; it's just a matter of practice. We'll cover more patterns in chapter six.

Related But on Steroids

The second major way to spot the Olympic long-jump gap between the evidence and the conclusion is to see if the conclusion is making a strong or extreme claim from the evidence. I like to think of these claims as if they are on steroids. Ask yourself, is it on the "juice?" First, if the evidence is actually talking about the same concepts as in the conclusion, then you don't have to worry about finding a "relevant" assumption answer choice.

For example, in the Rolex argument there was "luxury" in the evidence and "profits" in the conclusion, and clearly you needed to find an answer choice that shortened the Olympic gap between these two mismatched terms by saying that luxury = profits.

What if, however, the evidence and conclusion don't have terms that appear to be thrown in from nowhere? What if you're reading the argument and don't have to say, "Where did that come from?" In this scenario you then have to examine the evidence and conclusion and see if the conclusion that follows from the evidence is on steroids or not. For example, I might say, "A billboard ad on I-95 could triple my law firm's business, so it will ensure that I have a successful law firm." Did you see the power shift in the evidence, which states "could," to the conclusion, which states "will"?

Really? Something that could happen will happen? Unless you have a crystal ball or a time machine, it's not certain. The conclusion doesn't necessarily follow. It definitely could, but it doesn't have to. Every word on the LSAT serves a purpose; words are weapons. Use them appropriately. You'll

CLOSING THE GAP: FINDING THE ASSUMPTION

see a lot of these in the strengthen/weaken questions in the logical-reasoning section.

To weaken, just find an assumption that says, "I put an ad up and I lost business." This is especially true in causal arguments. Remember: on the LSAT, the author is claiming that nothing else caused Y to happen. There is nothing except a billboard ad that will ensure a successful law practice (i.e., the billboard ad and success are a married couple). To refute it, just find a counterexample (i.e., a "homewrecker") that denies it; negate it. Another way to weaken the assumption is to find something else that brought about having a successful law firm that wasn't caused by a billboard ad. How about word-of-mouth referrals? Instagram? Facebook? How about winning a major case that led you to be famous?

To strengthen the billboard-causing-success claim, eliminate all these alternative possibilities just mentioned; think of all other possibilities and negate it by adding a "not" in front of it, so it cannot happen. Something like "advertising on Instagram has been proven in a study to decrease (or not increase) the success of law firms." If any other option that can get you more business turns out to not work, then hey, billboards would be the ticket to success.

One small nuisance I discovered that test-makers love is that they obscure words by building in negatives or using double negatives, especially on harder questions. So instead of saying "not happy," they use words that have built-in negations such as "unhappy," which means the same thing. Alternatively, they can say "not unhappy," which means "happy." Be careful to not remove this answer choice just because you didn't explicitly see a "not."

Now, let's say that the evidence and conclusion are still talking about the same things (i.e., they are relevant), but instead of a conclusion being on steroids, the argument says something like: "If you advertise your law practice on a billboard, then you will have a successful law practice. Therefore, I have a successful law practice." Here the assumption in this conditional conclusion is you actually advertised, since that ensures a successful law practice (i.e., success is dependent upon your advertising).

Look for an answer choice that triggers the sufficient condition (advertising) or that triggers the contrapositive (i.e., If you are not successful, then you didn't advertise). Remember from chapter two that if you reverse the sufficient and condition statements or negate them without flipping them, then the answer simply Could Be True, not Must Be True; this is a common wrong-answer trap on the LSAT.

Another classic one, when the evidence and conclusion are relevant but the Olympic long jumper is still "sweating" hard, is when the conclusion gives you a prescription (i.e., it's recommending that you do or don't do something). How many times have you told someone or has someone told you that you "should" or "should not" do something because of reason XYZ? For example, you should advertise your law firm on a billboard because your law firm will get 200-300 leads a month on average.

Okay, this "should," or positive prescription, is putting

CLOSING THE GAP: FINDING THE ASSUMPTION

forth the idea that getting leads is more valuable than every other disadvantage of advertising on the billboard. What if it's too expensive and I don't get a return on my advertising budget? What if my reputation gets ruined because the ad was interpreted the wrong way by most people in town? What if people don't call? It's also saying that getting leads (i.e., this advantage) is more valuable than another competing advantage, such as getting 15 guaranteed customers. Maybe receiving 15 guaranteed customers is better than 200-300 leads (prospective customers) who could all potentially be people who never buy

Anytime you get a "should" or "should not," find the flip side to it. It's kind of like the particular "some" statements. If something could be true, it also could be false. If the argument was "you should not advertise your law firm on the billboard because it's expensive," the assumption is overlooking the fact that maybe the leads you will get will pay a dividend greater than the costs of advertising. It's basically saying that this won't happen. But remember, it could; what could be false could also be true.

A very common way in which the evidence falls apart on the road to the conclusion is when the argument presents the classic "correlation versus causation" claim, which is displayed numerous times throughout the LSAT; the evidence is saying that two things are correlated, so therefore A caused B. For example, for every month I advertised with a billboard on I-95 I got 300 new phone-call leads. Therefore, the billboard caused the leads to roll in. The assumption here is that nothing else caused me to get 300 new leads. Not my

Instagram, not my Facebook account, not my winning the big case a month before, etc.

However, maybe it was just a coincidence. For example, say that the next month I did it I got only 100 leads. When you see a correlation in the evidence and a cause claim in the conclusion (A causes B), think about the author saying that nothing else in the world can cause B other than A: not the reverse (B causing A) or not an alternative scenario (D causing both A and B)—nothing.

To weaken the claim, simply find an alternative cause or show that when you advertised on the billboard (i.e., did A) it did not lead you to get 300 leads (i.e., did not cause B). You might have only gotten 100 leads. Think of causal arguments as a happily married couple; the billboard and leads always go together and you cannot break them apart. If you do, you just weakened the argument. In other words, find the home-wrecker.

Okay, a final way to spot if the conclusion follows from the evidence is by seeing if the evidence talks about something in the past and then claims that that thing will happen in the future. For example, for the past 30 years I advertised on the billboard and my price never has changed; therefore, next year it won't change either. Well, we don't necessarily know that, right? It may not change, or it may.

The assumption is that the past pricing remains static indefinitely. Or the argument could say that in the past 30 years the billboard advertising prices changed every year, so next year it definitely will change. This time the assumption is that change will always happen. Again, that's not necessarily true. Thus, look for the answer choice that highlights this past-versus-future assumption.

Once you master how a conclusion doesn't necessarily follow by these patterns, you will be able to crush the logical-reasoning sections. You will also see similar patterns of correct and incorrect answer choices after doing numerous practice tests. This was my biggest "a-ha" moment in my LSAT study grind. It took me a long time to understand how the evidence is relevant or not relevant and whether the conclusion necessarily follows or doesn't.

Before I used to agree or disagree with the evidence or just ignore it. Now I logically break down the argument in my mind by thinking about these Olympic jumps. I think "Okay, conclusion and evidence—relevant terms or not?" Okay, not relevant—fine. How can I shorten the Olympic long jumper's gap? I need to spot an assumption that makes the two somehow relevant, or less extreme, by introducing another possibility. Are the terms equal to each other or not equal? Is one dependent on another or is one generalizing to a larger class? This is how you make the evidence and conclusion click.

Next, think, "How can I close this gap and help my Olympic long jumper?" This is how you break down the logical-reasoning questions. Again, the context may be different, but the structure is all the same. Also keep in mind that these patterns are not mutually exclusive within themselves. They could overlap.

So, the biggest takeaway is to really look at the conclusion separate from the evidence and see how the author is trying to convince you to accept his or her claim. Put it in the standard argument form and figure out the assumption. Then, you have the power to spot it, strengthen it, weaken it, or match it to the appropriate flawed pattern. In other words, close the gap for the Olympic long jumper. Help him or her help you to reach for the gold: an LSAT score of 180.

EVIDENCE (RELEVANT OR NOT RELEVANT)?	CONCLUSION (IF RELEVANT—ON STEROIDS?)
Evidence talks about "luxury"	Conclusion talks about "profits"
Evidence talks about "not luxury"	Conclusion talks about "not profits"
Evidence talks about "my limited edition luxury Rolex Sky-Dweller"	Conclusion talks about "all luxury Rolex Sky-Dwellers"
Evidence says "could" happen	Conclusion says "will" happen
Evidence says "if advertise, then success"	Conclusion says "then successful"
Evidence says "ads = 300 leads a month"	Conclusion says "should advertise"
Evidence says "billboards ads & leads correlated?"	Conclusion says "billboards only way to get leads"
Evidence says "prices changed over the last 30 years"	Conclusion says "prices will change next year"

6

PASSIVE PATTERNS

On October 10, 2010, I ran my first full marathon (26.2 miles) in Chicago. Four months prior, I literally could not even run one mile. I was out of shape and had never run before in my life. Nevertheless, I decided that I had a goal to achieve, a bucket-list item to check off before turning 30, and so I was determined. In the beginning it was hard, conditioning my body to wake up early, doing two to three miles a day, alternating with four to six miles on the weekends, cooling off again during the weekdays, managing my time, etc.

But eventually, after I accomplished a couple of baby-step milestones, I believed in myself and the rest was history. My goal was to finish within the allocated time for the race, regardless of whether I finished first or even within the top 20 or 30 percent of the runners.

Training for and then running a marathon is very much like training for and then taking the LSAT. In the beginning I couldn't do more than 10 logical-reasoning questions, two reading-comprehension passages, or two logic games within the 35 minutes of allocated time if my life depended on it. Not to mention that out of those, I would only answer about 50% correctly. I remember my head spinning after reading some dense prose, a feeling similar to my body aching after running more than four miles. Just as I had no idea what an assumption was when I first started, I had no idea how to run (e.g., breathing appropriately, minimizing energy consumption, swinging arms correctly) or what to think while I was running.

It was about accomplishing one small baby step at a time, which built upon a solid foundation to tackle more LSAT problems within 35 minutes and to do more miles (under 10 minutes a mile) every week to have enough time to finish the race. As I got closer to the marathon I put more miles under my belt. As I got closer to the actual LSAT, I ramped up to doing more full five-section practice tests on Saturdays.

Both races (the LSAT and the marathon) are accomplishable, but take a lot of hard work and determination. They are both learnable. The question is: do you just want to finish the marathon within the allocated time, or do you want to do it under a certain time goal and beat the competition? Likewise, do you just want to get into any law school, or do you want to get into your desired law school and get some merit-based scholarship money to top it off?

After all, the business model of law schools is that the

lowest-scoring applicants' tuition covers the costs of the highest scorers. In other words, they give highest-scoring students "tuition discounts" or "scholarships" to recruit them to join their schools (while making the lowest scorers pay full price) so they can boost their rankings in publications such as *U.S. News and World Report.* So, with these facts in mind, the good news about taking the LSAT is that it's standardized (the answer choices and questions written are very similar from test to test); thus, it can be beaten. They cannot deviate much, if at all; otherwise it wouldn't be standard. Therefore, the first milestone you need to tackle is learning the common patterns across the test. I call these the "passive patterns" because the test makers will throw the same patterns over and over at you but change the context (i.e. it wont be blatantly obvious). Thus, you must train your mind to think about these immediately after reading the question or stimulus.

Conclusion Patterns

The first set of patterns you must learn are the conclusion patterns. Every argument, by definition, will have a conclusion that follows (strong, weak, or not at all) from the evidence. This is what real life is all about. People are always trying to persuade you that "you should do this," "the Feds will not raise interest rates," "his political views are bad," etc. So what are the most common conclusions? What is the main point of the argument? They usually fall into one of the following conclusions: prediction, prescription, relative comparison, and formal logic.

In addition, the level of certainty is also critical. It's either strong or weak. If the conclusion says "Jenny crushed the practice test last week, so she will most likely crush the real test next week," this is a weak prediction. The conclusion is using the hedging words "most likely." Furthermore, it's making a prediction by using the word "will". She will do something. Really?

What if she doesn't? Did she go to the future in her DeLorean time machine and come back to see if she actually did? If not, her conclusion is a weak prediction. If the conclusion says "Jenny will crush the real test next week," then it would be considered a strong prediction. What's the assumption? That what happens in the past will happen in the future, right? Now attack it. This is how you need to think to rock the LSAT.

A prescription is a conclusion that says, in so many words, "You should do something or not do something." When someone tells you in real life that you should do something, they are saying that the outcome recommended outweighs anything else. What they are overlooking is any potential downside. For example, let's take this conclusion: "You should buy a Ferrari; you have the money and you only live once." This is a strong positive recommendation. There are no hedging words, such as *likely*, *probably*, or *perhaps*, in the conclusion.

What if you go bankrupt and then can't afford the maintenance? What if it's the last edition of its kind and happens to get stolen and chopped up in pieces because each part is known to sell for $5,000-$10,000 on the black market? Any risk of a downside is overlooked. Thus, anytime you read a conclusion, say "no," and think about the immediate opposite and then other possibilities.

Next, let's say you have a relative comparison in the conclusion; this is when you compare two variables, such as "X versus Y." Let's take this example: "Doing a CrossFit workout is more likely to burn calories in one hour than working out at a non-CrossFit gym. This is a relative comparison conclusion, and a weak one. It uses the hedging words "more likely." Note that although it says "more likely," it's not 100% certain, as would be the case if we changed the words "is more likely to" to "will." Therefore, consider this conclusion weak.

When the conclusion involves the author siding with a piece of evidence, consider that evidence a fact. For example, let's say that the argument says: "Drinking Diet Coke could lead to ulcers because, in a study, those subjects who drank Diet Coke developed more ulcers than those who didn't drink it over the course of six months; therefore, drinking Diet Coke could be harmful to your health." Here you have the author siding with the fact that drinking Diet Coke leads to ulcers and could be harmful to your health (in the conclusion), but it's a weak siding. The author didn't conclude "will," but rather "could." Also note that, in this example, the evidence had a causal claim (those drinking Diet Coke developed more ulcers because of the Diet Coke), and the conclusion was agreeing or disagreeing with the evidence.

Remember: whatever is in the evidence cannot be disputed. If the evidence did not have a qualifier, such as *could* or *likely*, then it's a fact that is true. So, to weaken this argument you would want to introduce another possibility. Although they did develop more ulcers, that could have been due to the groups' age differences, eating habits, lifestyles, etc. Basically, show that there was something wrong with the study.

On the LSAT, each word is precisely provided to mean something and the test-makers will exploit each word to throw you off the road to your perfect 180 score. The question is: how many times will you be knocked out of the game before you are satisfied? Read each word very carefully; this is especially true in inference questions (to be discussed later).

Finally, here is a very common pattern you'll see on the LSAT (and in real life): If I do X, then Y happens. When the argument states that something is needed or depends upon something else, or uses the common "if-then" structure, it's a formal-logic conclusion. Since formal-logic conclusions are categorical by nature (i.e., they encompass "all" categories), they usually are strong. Here's an example: "If you want to make more money in your business than you did last year, you need to raise your prices." This is a strong if-then conclusion: raising your prices is *necessary* in order for you to make more money.

However, sometimes what follows the "then" part of the conditional statement could be a prediction, prescription, or relative comparison, which can be weak. Here's an example: "If you want to make more money in your business than you did last year, you will most likely have to raise your prices." Now this is a weak formal-logic conclusion because it's incorporating the weak qualifier "most likely" into the mix. To sum up breaking down conclusions, remember to identify the type of conclusions and then determine if it's strong or weak.

Spotting Conclusions Fast

One quick way to spot where the conclusion is an argument (especially on harder ones with no keywords) is to find the adverbs and adjectives: anything that ends in *-ly*, such as *clearly*, *obviously*, etc., or anything that describes a noun, such as *misguided*. In addition, opinionated words, such as *unfairly*, or any rebuttal that the author makes are very likely to be in the conclusion. For example, if the author states a critic's viewpoint by saying "some people believe . . ."and then says "however," you can almost anticipate the author's conclusion coming along.

Structurally, you will see "P (conclusion) followed by Q (evidence)," or if you see a colon (:), then whatever is before the colon is usually the conclusion and whatever is after the colon is usually the evidence. It took me a very long time and lots of practice tests to see these patterns and now, when I see an argument, I'm immediately attracted to these conclusion indicators, which I can then use to "reverse engineer" and work backwards to find the support and then the assumption.

Types of Conclusions and Keywords:

- Prediction: *will, will not, would be, would not*
- Prescription: *should, should not, ought to, ought not*
- Relative comparison: *A versus B, A over B, words ending in -er*
- Formal Logic: *If X happens, then Y follows; the Y plan is needed or the Y plan will most likely be needed, is essential, only by*

Level-of-Certainty Keywords:

- Strong (has no qualifier words): *will, is, must, will be, does not, have not, we can, should, should not*

- Weak, with hedging language (has qualifier words): *likely, sometimes, most likely, tends to, possibly, perhaps, will most likely, very likely, might*

Now, once you locked up the conclusion type and the strength of it, you need to filter through the argument and find the evidence. In more complicated arguments you will have various pieces of sentences that appear to support your conclusion. It's imperative to filter out the "noise" or filler material and find the piece of evidence (or two) to evaluate so you can determine if the conclusion necessarily follows.

Now, what can you use to support your recommendations? How are you supporting your thesis? Why should I donate money to your cause? Convince me. How are you going to convince me? What's the method? This is what the evidence is all about. It's the premises in the argument that state the "why" you should do or not do my conclusion.

Evidence Patterns

So here are the patterns of evidence or the "passive patterns" for how to argue. Caution: don't try this at home; your friends and significant others will get really mad. The jump between evidence and conclusion can be huge (MBF), small (CBT/CBF), or nonexistent (MBT). Once you use the evidence to point to the conclusion, you need to make sure it's airtight (as discussed in chapter three); otherwise, it will be primed for attack. Thus, all methods below will point to the evidence necessarily or not necessarily. Some could be true, some could be false, some not possible at all (flaw), and some will always be true.

How to Argue Using Evidence:

- Citing examples
- Using experts
- Listing all possibilities and eliminating all but yours
- Stating that something is needed
- Using a similar situation, such as an analogy
- Stating a principle or broad rule (using formal logic)
- Using past data to support future data
- Using counterexamples to attack the speaker
- Ignoring the speaker's evidence and replacing it with your own evidence to arrive at the same conclusion
- Using the speaker's evidence but arriving at a different conclusion
- Attacking the speaker's argument via a counterexample (negating via a specific case)
- Attacking the speaker, not the argument
- Using tons of particular case studies to support a generalization
- Using correlation to arrive at a conclusion
- Using causation and agreeing or disagreeing with it.

As you can see, some pieces of evidence relate to supporting your own claim and some methods discuss supporting your rebuttal of the speaker's claim. Some pieces of evidence are flawed, such as using various particular cases to generalize to an entire group of people, or attacking the speaker's character as opposed to the argument itself (seen frequently in political ads), or, more commonly seen on the LSAT, using two independent events in the evidence and claiming that one caused the other in the conclusion.

On the other hand, some pieces of evidence that are irrefutable, or Must Be True, occur when the evidence has a categorical, formal-logic statement (an "all or none" statement) leading to a necessary conclusion (See the classroom example in chapter three). When you see the following patterns in the evidence of formal logic there's only one correct answer (along with its contrapositive) for the conclusion to necessarily follow; anything other than this is a flaw.

Valid Argument Patterns

For valid arguments, the conclusion must be true 100% of the time from the evidence:

Every M is P.
Every S is M.

Therefore, every S is P.

If A, then B
A

Therefore, B

If A, then B
~B

Therefore, ~A (contrapositive)

No Ps are Cs.
Every S is a P.

Therefore, no Ss are Cs.

With categorical statements you need to combine the duplicate terms in the premises to make a deduction; it's like playing connect-the-dots (or logic games). Trace your way from the sufficient terms to the necessary terms throughout the argument. You can only combine terms when the results of one statement (the right side of the arrow) match the sufficient term of another statement (the left side of the arrow).

IF A → **B**

IF **B** → C

Therefore, A → **B** → C

If **A** → B

If C → **A**

Therefore, C → **A** → B

Sufficient Assumption Patterns

If there are no duplicate terms distributed throughout the middle between both pieces of evidence, or premises, the best you can deduce is the following. When both terms in the evidence are found on the sufficient side (left side of the arrow):

IF **P** → Q

IF **P** → W

Therefore, **P** → Q and W

When both terms in the evidence are found on the necessary side (right side of the arrow):

> IF T → W
>
> IF P → W
>
> Therefore, T or P (or both) → W

What's very important to note is that when both duplicate terms are aligned on either the sufficient side or the necessary side (i.e., there is no shared duplicate on the opposite side), then you have found out what is missing to make a logical link. You would need to create a *middle shared term*. In the above example, since "W" is on the necessary side in both premises, you need to create a piece of evidence that match P and T together.

This is considered your sufficient assumption. It's considered sufficient because it's more than enough to prove the conclusion without a doubt. For example, if the assumption was "if P, then T," you can insert that into the argument to prove the conclusion beyond a doubt:

Argument's missing sufficient assumption (as-is):

> IF T → W
>
> IF P → W **(conclusion)**

Notice how the right side of the arrows is duplicated with "W." You now need to find a piece of evidence to match up the left side of the arrows (connecting P to T) to arrive at a Must Be True conclusion. Right now you cannot combine or connect the dots to make a claim, such as "if T, then W." There's no middle term to trace. You need to create it:

The "U" Pattern

Argument with "left" sufficient assumption pattern (connecting P to T):

IF P → T (assumption)
IF T → W

Therefore, P → W

The same goes with the necessary side. You now need to find a piece of evidence to match up the right side of the arrows (connecting Q to W) to arrive at a Must Be True conclusion. Right now you cannot combine or connect the dots to claim "if P, then W." There's no middle term to trace. You need to create it:

Argument's missing sufficient assumption:

IF P → Q

IF P → W (conclusion)

The Reverse "U" Pattern
An argument with the "right" sufficient assumption pattern (connecting Q to W):

IF P → Q
IF **Q** → W (assumption)

Therefore, P → W

Between every piece of evidence and the conclusion is the assumption that is most vulnerable. It's the unstated piece of evidence that makes the conclusion and the evidence lock together. It's the missing piece of the jigsaw puzzle. Thus, to make the evidence lock in with the conclusion, you must tighten up the assumption by removing alternative possibilities, using deductive reasoning, etc.

The Block Method: "Some" and "Most" Statements

One last pattern I discovered during the countless hours of LSAT prep was the use of particular or "some" and "most" statements (*some, few, many, most, at least*) in the evidence to arrive at a conclusion. This is tested heavily on inference, or Must Be True, logical-reasoning questions. These questions generally don't have an argument (no reasoning, or "why," for the evidence). Your entire goal is to decipher the quantity (some or all) from the argument to see if the conclusion necessarily follows (100% of the time).

Here some patterns to note. First, when there are two "some" statements in the evidence, you cannot arrive at a valid Must Be True conclusion. Since a "some" statement is reversible, you don't know which particular case is being talked about.

Some Ms are Ps.
Some Ws are Ms.

Therefore, No Valid Conclusion (NVC).

Sure, it's possible that "Some Ws are Ps" (tracing left to right in both premises from W to P) but it's not necessarily so. To illustrate this, list out the entities in the block method. Take each premise and list out the variables. Repeat for the next premise. Then visually see if the conclusion necessarily follows or not. For example:

1. Some Ms are Ps: **PMPM**PPPPPPPP (This shows that two Ms ["some"] are P.)

2. Some Ws are Ms: **PMWPMW**PPPPPPPP (This shows that two Ws ["some"] are Ms.)

3. However, there are tons of Ps unaccounted for (PPPPP); therefore, you cannot make a 100% claim that some Ps are Ms. Sure, it could be true that some Ps are Ms, but it's also true that some Ps are not Ms, as you can see from the non-highlighted portion, making the claim a Could Be True answer (i.e., invalid) instead of a Must Be True answer (i.e. valid).

Second, when there is a "some" statement in the evidence, you cannot use it as support for an "all" statement in the conclusion. This is the part-to-whole fallacy. The quantity (all) in the conclusion cannot exceed the quantity (some) in the premise. Just become some people do X doesn't mean all people will do X. Conversely, if the conclusion is a universal term (all, none), then there has to be at least one premise with a universal term as well.

Another example, going back to our cat-walkers from chapter three, is:

Some Cs (cat lovers) are Ps (walk cats).
Some Bs (bodybuilders) are Cs (cat lovers).

Therefore: No Valid Conclusion

Cat Lovers

Bodybuilders   Walk Cats

[   ]

Just because some bodybuilders are cat lovers and some cat lovers walk cats doesn't mean that all or some bodybuilders walk cats. They would be "guilty by association." Notice how there is a gap between bodybuilders and walking cats in the diagram above (see brackets). Thus, you can't draw a valid conclusion. Now, let's put this into the block method:

1. Some Cs are Ps: **PCPC**PPPPPPPP (This shows that two Cs ["some"] are Ps.)

2. Some Bs are Cs: **PCBPC**PPPPPPPP (This shows that one B ["some"] is a C.)

3. However, there is one PC, as well as tons of Ps unaccounted for (PPPPP); therefore, you cannot make a 100% certain claim that some Bs are Ps. Sure, it could be true that some Bs are Ps, but it's also true that some Bs are not Ps, as you can see from the non-highlighted portion, making the claim a Could Be True answer (i.e., invalid) as opposed to a Must Be True answer (i.e., valid).

Also note if you have a "some" statement as a conclusion then there has to be a "some" statement in the evidence along with an categorical, or "all," statement.

If M, then H.
Some Hs are Ks.

Therefore, **some** Ms are Ks (valid): MH**MHKMHK**

Here all Ms are Hs, every single one of them. And some Hs (lets say two, as highlighted above) are Ks. Well, if every single M is a K, it must be true that the two Hs that were attached to K are now attached to M. Thus, some Ms are Ks is a Must Be True conclusion.

Remember: the quantity in the conclusion (e.g., all) cannot exceed the quantity of the premise (e.g., some). Finally, pay attention to the tone of the argument (positive or negative). If the conclusion has a negative (not) claim, then the premise must have at least one negative statement.

No Ps are Cs.
Every S is a P.

Therefore, **no** Ss are Cs (valid).

When you have a negative term, always take the contrapositive and link up the chain. For example, "No Ps are Cs" translates to "If P, then not C."

If **P**, then ~C.
If S, then **P**.
___
IF S, then ~C (Must Be True).

Another common pattern involves "most" statements. Remember that a "most" statement means more than half (i.e., 51 to 100). Also, if something is "most," that implies it's also "some"; "all" implies "most," which implies "some." Therefore, a "most" statement is often a "some" statement in disguise.

PASSIVE PATTERNS

If most people do something, then some people do it as well (going down the chain in logic). For example:

> **Most** As are Bs.
> **Most** As are Cs.
>
> Therefore, **some** Bs are Cs (valid).

Let's use the block method to break it down:

1. Most As are Bs: **BABABABA**AAA (This shows that four out of seven ["most"] As are Bs.)

2. Most As are Cs: BABABAB**ACACACAC** (This shows that four out of seven ["most"] As are Cs).

3. Therefore, there is one "BAC" in this world that must intersect and share paths BABABA**BAC**ACACAC, making "Some Bs are Cs" a valid (i.e., Must Be True) conclusion.

Making inferences or deductions is as simple as tracing and combining. It's really not that complicated. Simply find the truth; figure out what Must Be True.

Universal and Particular Statements Summary

- If premises are universal (e.g., all), the conclusion must also be universal (e.g., all).
- If the term in the conclusion is universal (e.g., none), then the same term must be universal in the premise (e.g., none).
- Conclusions must reflect the quality (positive/negative) of the premises. If the conclusion is negative, then there must be one premise that's negative.
- The quantity (all vs. some) of a term that appears in the conclusion (e.g., all) must not exceed the quantity of the same term as it appears in the premise (e.g., some).
- Any term distributed in the conclusion must be distributed in the premises.
- The middle term must be distributed in at least one of the premises to lead to a conclusion.
- Two "some" statements equals an invalid conclusion.
- "Some" statements are reversible (Some R are Q = Some Q are R).
- When in doubt, use the block method to figure what Must Be True.

The logical-reasoning section makes up most of your score on the LSAT. Thus, it's the most important section. The LSAT writers test your ability to think about reasoning structure, not content. Therefore, to bag the maximum amount of points, it's imperative to separate the conclusion from the evidence and ask if it necessarily follows (100%). Since it's on the LSAT it most likely will not, so then you must determine if what's supporting the conclusion is relevant or not.

If it's not relevant, match up the terms that are thrown out of "left field" together. If it is relevant, figure out if the conclusion is on steroids. Both methods are known as discovering your assumption. Once you have the assumption or "missing link," identify it, destroy it, augment it, or match it to the appropriate flaw pattern. Also think about the strength of the premises and conclusion to see if they are weak (i.e., if it uses qualifiers such as *may, could,* or *likely*) or strong (i.e., if it doesn't use qualifiers but rather strong statements such as *will* or *must*).

Finally consider the quantity of the statements. For example, do the premises use particular or "some" statements to draw a universal or "all" conclusion? If so, you have then you found the flaw: it's unrepresentative. Now that you can break down any argument, let's turn to the different question types you will see in the logical-reasoning section and drill the specific strategies for each. So, sharpen your #2 pencils, grab a latte, and let's get started.

7

THE TRICKS OF THE TRADE IN LOGICAL-REASONING QUESTIONS

You turn the page to section one of the LSAT and you see 24-26 of the longest short arguments you will ever see in your life. The very first thing you must do is figure out what each question is asking you. Once you identify what question "type" it is, figure out how far the Olympic long jump is from the evidence to the conclusion. For example, in a flaw question, the entire argument is corrupted. The jump is impossible, so you just have to spot which type of flaw it is because you cannot repair the argument.

With a strengthen/weaken argument, the jump is long but you can shorten it for the Olympian by giving him or her props to get to the other side (i.e., strengthening the argument). Conversely, you can make the jump harder by

THE TRICKS OF THE TRADE IN LOGICAL-REASONING QUESTIONS

making the disconnected evidence and conclusion further apart (i.e., weakening the argument). Or you can simply just identify the missing link (i.e., the assumption), and use cement to make the conclusion necessarily follow from the evidence using the perfect patterns discussed in chapter six.

So, the minute your pencil touches the paper, the first thought in your head should be what type of question you're looking at (see Appendix B). Next: is there an argument or only facts? If there is an argument, where is the conclusion? Where is the evidence? Does the conclusion necessarily follow? No; okay, is the evidence relevant? No; okay, so match the two unrelated concepts (e.g., luxury and profits) in the evidence and conclusion. If the evidence is related to the conclusion and no matching needs to be done, is the conclusion on steroids (i.e., using extreme language such as *must, only,* or *primarily*)?

Okay, so what is a possible scenario the author overlooked? Let's say that the police said that I must have killed someone because a witness saw me and no one else coming out of Starbucks, where the body was found dead around the same time in the back alley. Really—I must have? Maybe I was sipping my latte at Starbucks and someone dumped the body next to Starbucks while I was walking out. Maybe someone else killed him. Maybe the witness killed him and is pointing fingers at the competition (me) so he can inherent the deceased's fortune. Deny everything, point out several possibilities, and create tons of doubt. That's how you "go to bat" for your client when his or her life and entire life savings are on the line in your escrow account.

Now, if it's not an argument, then you are only dealing with facts. In this scenario you're not asked to be critical of the argument, but rather to focus on the structure of the stimulus. For example, seeing how a particular sentence functions within the stimulus, explaining a discrepancy between two sets of facts, identifying the main point (nothing more), or combining sentences and forming contrapositives to deduce what Must Be True.

Below is a mental thinking script that you should print out and have next to you when you are attacking logical-reasoning "LR" questions. The more questions you completed under your belt, the faster you can drill this thinking script in your mind so it becomes second nature, just like driving.

Seven Questions to Attack Logical-Reasoning Arguments

If an argument is present then . . . .

1. Read the question stem.
2. What's the task (identify flaw, identify assumption, strengthen, weaken, etc.)?
3. Identify the conclusion (i.e., main point)? Bracket this.
4. Identify the support (i.e., evidence)? Underline this.
5. Think what's wrong with the support leading to the conclusion (Is it not related or on steroids?). Write this assumption down.
6. Predict the correct answer choice by tasks. For example, if it's a weaken question introduce an alternative possibility. If it's a strengthen question, add a "not" to

an alternative possibility (i.e., negate the assumption). If it's a sufficient-assumption question, pick a powerful assumption that guarantees the conclusion (with extreme language). Think about "U" and reverse the "U" pattern. If it's a necessary-assumption question, choose a soft assumption (i.e., one without extreme language) that the conclusion depends on. So, if you deny it then it negates the conclusion (i.e., makes it fall apart). Denying a "some statement" (1-100) is saying it can't happen—"none (0)." If you say now this cannot happen, then if the argument falls apart it is the correct necessary assumption. If there's a flaw, match it to a specific flaw pattern, as there's no repairing the argument.
7. Eliminate wrong answers (e.g., doesn't match your prediction, which can be not relevant; extreme language; a distortion; focuses on a wrong viewpoint, etc.) and select the answer choice that has the most support by the stimulus.

Seven Questions to Attack Logical-Reasoning Non-Arguments

If only facts are present then . . . .

1. Figure out the question type.
2. What's the task? (Explain the discrepancy? Infer an MBT or MBF? Identify the conclusion or evidence?)
3. If it's an inference question, eliminate extreme (*all*, *none*,

most statements) or anything not mentioned or supported in the stimulus. Also, combine and form contrapositives
4. If asked to explain the discrepancy, ask "How can both A and B work?" Eliminate any answer choice that deepens the mystery or only explains one side.
5. If asked to identify the main point, look for the author's rebuttals and opinionated words such as *should* or *will*, or any words that end in "-ly."
6. Eliminate wrong answer choices first and narrow your choices down to two options.
7. Put your finger on the sentence in the stimulus that supports the correct answer choice and select it. This answer choice must be proven by the stimulus.

Now, with the proper framework in mind, let's touch on best-practice quick strategies for the different question types you will see on the LSAT. Note that you will want to practice these strategies by question type (e.g., doing 20 flaw questions back to back) so it's best to purchase a logical-reasoning book by question type online.

How to Paraphrase Dense Arguments

Before starting, it's important to make a distinction as to what makes a logical reasoning question hard. Usually, it will be that you simply don't understand what the stimulus, or question, or answer choice is saying. Test-makers create this effect by putting unnecessary information into the argument

THE TRICKS OF THE TRADE IN LOGICAL-REASONING QUESTIONS

(i.e., contextual information) to confuse you. So, the more confused you are, the more time you spend on the question and the greater likelihood of your getting the problem wrong due to the compounding effect of the time pressure.

Therefore, the very first thing you should do is practice understanding the stimulus by putting it in your own words. There are two main ways to do this. First, you can take out a Word document and type the argument, after you read it, in your own words. The key is to not use any words verbatim from the stimulus. So, label the conclusion and premises, and figure out the assumption in that order.

The key is to look for the conclusion keywords (*thus, therefore, so*, etc.) and read backwards. If the conclusion is prescribing something, ask "Why?" Then type in the supporting evidence (i.e., the premises) and figure out if the two are related or not. If they are related, then look to see if the argument is on steroids. Don't solve the problem; rather, just do this for the question types in the section and then go back and try to solve the entire set (e.g., 25 questions) from your Word doc.

The other way is turn your paper over and physically write out these same things. Although typing will take longer, I found that typing forcing you to focus more and helps with retention. Regardless, either way is fine. They both will help you really get a grasp on figuring out what the argument says. Here's an example of what my Word document or paper would look like with a logical-reasoning section. "C" is for conclusion, "E" is for evidence or combined premises (try to combine all the support into one major premise), and "A" is for assumption.

Q1. C: Birds and infants same genes; E: B/C look alike; A: nothing other than appearance = same genes; looking alike only reason.
Q2. Repeat
Q3. Repeat

Once you master the skill of paraphrasing, then you can dive into the questions and rip them apart. The logical-reasoning questions will be broken down into argument-based or non-argument-based (i.e., just facts). If the stimulus doesn't have a conclusion (opinion) and evidence (the "why"), then you have only facts and don't have to be critical of the stimulus. With only facts, your job is to identify something, explain something, or make deductions (i.e., chaining *all*, *most*, and *some* statements together and finding out what Must Be True).

As discussed before with inference problems, trace your way home. Find duplicate words in different sentences, combine them, take the contrapositive, and look for the Must Be True answer. In other words, you have to stick to the facts. If the entire stimulus says "some," it doesn't mean "most." No ad-libbing allowed. Below are the best practices for each question type. Do at least 10 questions back to back by question type to really drill in the foundation listed below. Also, I recommend making note cards directly from these below. For example, put "Inference Questions" on the front and on the back put "correct" and "incorrect" for strategy.

THE TRICKS OF THE TRADE IN LOGICAL-REASONING QUESTIONS

BEST PRACTICES BY QUESTION TYPE: NON-ARGUMENTS

Inference Questions (MBT, MBF)

Keywords in Question Stem: must be true, logically completes, conclusion that can be properly drawn, leads to which conclusion, concluded from the statements above, can be expected as a result, inference that can be drawn, properly inferred, could be true except, must be false, must be true except

Summary: No argument. Align sentences from categorical to particular (*all, most, some*). If there are two *some* statements and two *all* statements, rearrange the statements on paper. Place the *all* statements on top of the *some* statements so you can trace your way to the correct answer choice. Remember: the correct logical chain for a Must Be True answer is *all-most-some*, going downward. So, if the stimulus says "if A, then B" you know that means "if A, then maybe B," since A guaranteeing B (i.e., a *will/must*) implies *might, could,* and *maybe*. In contrast, if it says "if A then maybe B," you cannot infer it *must* imply B as you cannot go up the logic chain from *some-most-all*.

Next, spot duplicate words in sentences. Combine and conclude a Must Be True or Must Be False. Find an answer choice supported by the text. For example, if "risk" was mentioned in premise one and then again in premise three, you can combine these statements and take the contrapositive. So if the right answer is "if X then Y," the LSAT will show "if not Y, then not X." This is the correct answer.

I like to think of inference questions as logic games.

Your job is to find out what Must Be True and separate it from what Could Be True and Must Be False. This is exactly what you are being tested on with this question type in the logical-reasoning section. For Must Be False questions (i.e., questions that say "could be true except"), the correct answers will negate the inference deduced from the stimulus. So, if you inferred "all cold drinks are wet," find an answer choice that says that some cold drinks are not wet.

Wrong Answer Choices: Mainly, these are extreme (i.e., use words such as *none, only, the only, depends, main, primarily, all, never,* most, etc.) and are not supported by the text (e.g., adds new info). If you can't point your finger to the three or four sentences in the stimulus then it's not the correct answer. The typical wrong answers on inference questions are answer choices that Could Be True but are not necessarily true (100%). They'll do this by starting at the wrong side of the chain of logic. For example, if A ➔ B ➔ C the answer choice will say "If C ➔ A." Remember that a Must Be True answer must work from left to right (not in reverse). Also, they will negate the sufficient condition and see if you fall for that trap: "If ~ A ➔ C."

Also, if there is a weird "out of left field" term in the answer choice and the set of facts in the stimulus never mentions it—toss it out. For example, if the facts are talking about "sales" and all of a sudden an answer choice mentions "profit," it's irrelevant. (Test-makers love to do this.) You should be able to point your finger to the sentence and see exactly where the answer choice is supported by the set of facts. Also, any relative comparison made in the answer choices that's not supported or mentioned is generally wrong as well (e.g., A more effective than B). Finally, there will be an answer choice that will directly contradict a statement.

For example, if one statement says "all bees like honey" (B → H), the answer choice will say "Some bees do not like honey (B some ~ H)." You simply do not know. Finally, watch out for tricky wording such as "each of many X do Y"; this is nothing more than an "all" statement. They throw "many" after "each" to make you think it's a "some" statement. For example: "Each of 50 people who ate ice cream" is still talking about 50 people who ate ice cream.

The correct answer must always be supported by the fact set; stick very close to the text. In Must Be True questions, Could Be False (i.e., you don't know if the statement is true or false) and Must Be False (i.e., directly contradicting sentences) statements are wrong. Ask yourself, "How do I know this? Is it proven by the above?" Remember: you're being tested on your fact-finding skills, not your reasoning skills. This holds true also for the reading-comprehension section. You must be able to say, "Line 55 specifically says sales" and confidently pick the answer choice. The biggest and deadliest trap with inference questions is relying on memory.

"Most Strongly Support" Questions

Keywords in Question Stem: most strongly supported, most strongly inferred, analogy can best be understood, statements above support the view, above provides most support for which one of the following hypotheses, which of the following inferences is most strongly supported, which conclusion below is best supported by the statements above.

Summary: No argument. Answer choices will have the conclusion you need to infer from facts in the stimulus (i.e., the premises). It's similar to a main-point question. The answer choice can come just from one line of text in the stimulus. The answer choice doesn't have to be 100% valid, just most strongly supported (99%). A common pattern is to mention a specific item in the stimulus (e.g., a basketball player does X), and then the answer choice says something like "Basketball players do X." Think in terms of: all supports most and some. Always point your figure back to the passage or line item to make sure that answer choice is supported. Ask yourself when evaluating answer choices: "How do I know this? Is it proven by the above?" Remember: you're being tested on your fact-finding skills, not your reasoning skills.

For questions that with the words *least or* except, you're looking for four answer choices that support and one that does not, which is usually irrelevant. For example, if the stimulus were talking about mammals and one answer choice talks about "non-mammals," then that would be the correct answer. Since you don't know anything about non-mammals, you can't know for certain if it's supported or not supported; thus, it's the correct answer.

Wrong Answer Choices: These are mainly extreme (i.e., use words such as: *none, only, depends, main, primarily, all, never,* etc.) and not supported by the text (e.g., add new info). If you can't point your finger to the three or four sentences in the stimulus, then it's not the correct answer. For example, if the stimulus talks about people who drink coffee and the answer choice mentions those who don't drink coffee, that cannot be proven (i.e., it Could Be False) and it's therefore wrong. Also, any irrelevant comparisons made (A versus B) that are not mentioned in the stimulus, but are in the answer choices, are wrong. Finally, any answer choice that contradicts a line in the stimulus is wrong as well. If the stimulus says "will not lose weight" and an answer choice says "will lose weight" by removing a "not," it is wrong.

Resolve/Explain Questions

Keywords: *resolve, explain, reconcile, apparent discrepancy, anomaly*

Summary: No argument. Two facts are provided that appear contradictory but are not after a second glance. Separate both parts of the stimulus. Find one piece of evidence that makes both sentences work. Think, "Why does X happen but then Y doesn't? or "Why can't X do Y, but Z can do Y?" The correct answer choice will explain why both facts are different. When going through the answer choices, ask yourself, "Does this answer choice explain the puzzle?" Let's look at an example: "Recent research found that burning 1000 calories a day while eating only 1500 calories a day will result in rapid weight loss; however, a group of participants who participated in a study for 30 days actually gained weight." Here, you need an answer choice that links up the contradictory set of statements. For example, although the calories consumed were 1500 a day, they were mainly from saturated fat, which is the equivalent of eating double the amount of calories from lean protein.

Since all the answer choices will be tempting, after reading the discrepancy take a second, and ask yourself, "Why is it that___?" or "How can this be?" Write that prediction out next to the question and scan the answer choices for it. This is how you save time and stay in control instead of being enticed by each answer choice. I like to think of these questions as being like flaw questions. You know the leap between evidence and conclusion is impossible; however, your job is to figure out a piece of evidence or a fact set that can make everything fit in as a big happy family. Also, for explaining "except" questions you will have four answer choices that will explain or reconcile how both sets of facts work together and one that does not; usually this answer choice is irrelevant and makes you say, "So what?"

Wrong Answer Choices: Focus on only one set of facts; resolve only one side or make the paradox more puzzling. If, after you read each answer choice, you say, "And, so what?" then each of those answers did not explain the phenomena in question. Basically, you need a fact that makes both contradictory statements work. What you don't want to do is pick an answer choice that deepens the mystery or is irrelevant to the fact set (e.g., talks about not dieting when the fact set is about dieting). The LSAT test-makers love to do this as well. They give you facts about smokers, for example, and then mention non-smokers in the answer choices.

Principle Example (Rule on the Bottom) Questions
Keywords: Which principle, rule, or generalization below most helps to justify X?

Summary: No argument. Understand the example in the

stimulus and match it to a rule in the answer choices below (i.e., on the bottom). Ask whether the stimulus can serve as an example of rules A, B, C, D, or E. For example, if the stimulus says that Kyle was guilty of stealing because he walked out of a store with the tag still on his shirt, your conclusion is: he's guilty. The evidence is: the tag was still on. Your job is to find a rule that makes the two connect. Something like "Anyone who has their tags still on their shirt while walking out is guilty of stealing." Now, go hunt for the correct answer choice. Check each answer choice against each part of the rule to validate why it's wrong or right.

A principle is a conditional statement (If P → Q). The stimulus will provide you with a scenario that you must match to the correct rule in the answer choices. One quick way to do these problems is to quickly scan the necessary conditions in the answer choices to see if there are any rule contradictions with the example above. If so, quickly eliminate and then evaluate the answer choices starting from the bottom up. Since they are structurally easy to see, these are easier than other question types.

Wrong Answer Choices: Don't focus on matching the points, rules, or the sufficient or necessary part of the rule. For example, if the stimulus says "if A then B," they will provide "not A" as the answer choice (i.e., fail the sufficient condition), which cannot be correct. Also, wrong answers will have similar subjects but illustrate a different rule. Also, they will mention an incorrect rule or secondary rule. Furthermore, they will negate the rule. If the rule says "A, therefore B," the wrong answer choice will say, "A, therefore not B." That can never be, as it goes against the rule, so you can quickly eliminate that answer choice. Also, the stimulus may have a qualifier such as " X may want Z" and then the answer choice says "X was successful at getting Z," which becomes unsupported.

BEST PRACTICES BY QUESTION TYPE: ARGUMENTS

Main-Point-Conclusion Questions
Keywords: *main point, main conclusion, point made, X in support of the claim that*

Summary: Argument. Your task is to simply identify or label the author's conclusion (i.e., very opinionated words), which is usually a prescription (e.g., the author stating what should or should not be done) or a rebuttal after another viewpoint in the stimulus (e.g., "some scientists believe . . ."); the other person's viewpoint actually foreshadows the conclusion.

For example, if the viewpoint says, "if X, then Y" and the author says "however" or "but," then you know he's not agreeing with that statement, meaning, "if X *then not* Y." Here, think "what" versus "why" to arrive at the correct answer. You're not being asked why the author concludes X but rather simply what X is. All you're doing is identifying the conclusion. Once you find it, stop reading and jump to the answer choices. A common pattern is XYZ (conclusion) because (W) evidence or because X (evidence), Y (conclusion).

Scan quickly for the keywords *but* and *since* and the conclusion will be either after or before both. Also, look for words that end in an adverb (e.g., clearly, accordingly, etc.).

Also, very opinionated words (e.g., X is misled), adjectives (e.g., *large* appetite), rare verbs/nouns, and short sentences are signs of conclusions. Other clues are *it follows that, it is clear that, for this reason*, etc. These phrases signal a conclusion.

On difficult main-point questions, try to pre-phrase the conclusion in your own words and jot it down and then ask "Why?" If you can find the "why" or reasoning after the sentence (indicated by *since* or *because*), you know it's the correct conclusion because you need support to back up the claim. Also, if you're really stuck say to yourself, "Would the author agree to this answer choice?" If yes, then that is the main conclusion. Finally, ask yourself, "If there were only one sentence I would wish to keep in the stimulus, what would it be?" This will help you narrow down the main point of the argument. The biggest thing to remember is that you're just being asked to identify or label the conclusion, not to criticize it.

Wrong Answer Choices: Focus on evidence or another person's viewpoint. Extreme answers that take the main point out of proportion are similar traps (e.g., ones that start with *no one, always, must, never*, etc.). If the answer choice focuses on anything that follows *for, also, because*, etc., you know it's the evidence and cannot be a conclusion. Go back to the stimulus and see if that answer choice has the evidence keywords starting the sentence. If that sentence begins with *also*, for example, that answer choice is not the main conclusion.

For every sentence you read, ask if it's background info, evidence, a sub-conclusion, or the main conclusion. Read for structure and soon conclusions will pop out easily. The really hard main points will have several sub-conclusions in them.

To achieve mental clarity, always ask yourself "What is the main point?" or "Why is my time being wasted with this?" This will be the conclusion.

Pay very close attention to who is talking. Many of these questions will have different viewpoints (author, scientist, critic, etc.) and trap answers will have a restatement of evidence or the wrong person's conclusion waiting for you, sitting right on top of the correct main conclusion answer choice. Once again, the test-makers love setting you up for failure, so don't let them.

Strategy Role Questions

Keywords: *X plays which role, figures, functions, is used, serves in the argument in which of the following ways?*

Summary: Argument. Ask why the author included this fact or conclusion. What is it doing in the argument? Is the evidence stated to counter another viewpoint's evidence? Is the conclusion a subsidiary conclusion or the main conclusion? It's all about how the evidence is being used; what is the evidence doing? In an argument you have the main conclusion, sub-conclusions, evidence, and background information. The more dense arguments will double up and have sub-conclusions, two pieces of evidence, and more filler material to throw you off (e.g., introduce other viewpoints' arguments within the author's argument).

Also, there may be more than just the author's viewpoint; there may be a critic's viewpoint with its own evidence, conclusion, and noise. Therefore, next to each sentence make notes in shorthand (*ev, sub-c, m-conc, vpt1, bkg*) to keep track of who's saying what. Also, make sure you circle or bracket what you're being asked to identify in the stimulus.

So to efficiently attack these you must be able to quickly see if the "X statement" is the conclusion or evidence. If it's part of the conclusion, eliminate any answer choice that says *premise, supports the conclusion, evidence,* etc. If the LSAT requires you to zoom out and consider the evidence and conclusion from a top-down approach (versus just seeing the role of a few words), remember that you can only use the evidence to prove your point in so many ways: citing examples, using experts, listing all possibilities and eliminating all but yours, saying something is needed, stating a principle or broad rule, etc. Therefore, ask yourself, "How is this being argued?" Write that down and scan the answer choices to find a match for your prediction.

Wrong Answer Choices: Mix up the evidence and the conclusion or state another person's viewpoint as the correct answer. They also could state that a supposition (if-then hypothetical) is used to disprove a claim made in the argument, which cannot be as it's only a hypothetical. Another pattern is putting an "assumption" as the answer choice, which by definition can't be as an assumption as an assumption is unstated. A lot of strategy role questions have answer choices with extreme wording in them, such as *must, primary, crucial, no, disprove,* etc.

Strategy Technique Questions
Keywords: *responds to, proceeds by, argumentative strategy, argumentative techniques, how X responds, challenges,*

criticizes, counters, objects to Y, X derives its conclusion by, etc.

Summary: Argument. Ask how the author is arguing. How do the premises support the conclusion? Analogy? Providing examples and/or counter-examples? Listing three options and eliminating two? Citing a principle or rule? Generalizing backed by tons of case studies? Attacking the speaker? Ignoring the speaker's evidence? Using an expert? Using past data to support a future prediction? Using a cause in the evidence and agreeing with it in the conclusion? Saying something is necessary?

Always ask how the conclusion follows from the evidence. Focus on the structure and think how the author supports the conclusion. Also, the correct answer choice will have tons of modifiers and embedded language to keep the answer choices abstract, so you'll have to relate it back to the passage line by line.

Wrong Answer Choices: Focus on the main point of the argument instead of the structure.

Point-at-Issue Questions

Keywords: A and B disagree over . . . A and B agree over . . . What is the point at issue?

Summary: Argument. Two speakers make an argument and your job is to find what they are disagreeing or, on rare occasions, agreeing about. Let's say that, in real life, your friend starts talking about how traveling to Europe was the best experience they had, for example, and you start explaining how your experience was not all that great. During this conversation you have to both disagree over a certain piece of evidence or conclusion. Maybe you agree with the conclusion but don't agree with the evidence. Alternatively, maybe he or she agrees with your facts but arrives at a different conclusion.

So, we have separate conclusions and evidence in each argument. Look at conclusion first and ask if both have an opinion and if both disagree. If so, that is the answer. The answer choice must address both speakers' points. For example, if Jenny agrees with the answer choice because it says "beetles," but Josh never mentions anything about "beetles," then that cannot be the correct answer. Both speakers have to disagree over the answer choice. Therefore, figure out first if the disagreement (or agreement) is about the evidence or conclusion. Once you have that nailed down, you can eliminate several answer choices and then tune into the argument and figure out what it is about the facts or conclusion that they disagree over.

Check each answer choice against both the first and second person's argument and see if they both have an opinion about it and if they contrast to confirm the correct answer. It's best to use a "T-chart" and write "A V B Opinions" next to the answer choices (ABCDE). Read the first speaker's argument first (speaker A), separate the conclusion and the evidence, and then run down the answer choices and ask if that person had opinion on answer choice A, B, C, D, or E. If she has no opinion, eliminate it, because if there's no opinion, then you cannot disagree with that person.

For example, if the answer choice says "shielded" and speaker A doesn't use those words, then she does not have an opinion and therefore that answer choice needs to be eliminated. Repeat with the next speaker's argument (speaker B). If both speakers have an opinion, do they disagree? If so, that is the answer. In other words you want a triple "Y" for the correct answer: "YYY". Yes, speaker A has opinion; yes, speaker B has an opinion; and yes, they both disagree.

Wrong Answer Choices: Only state one person's (A or B) opinion, or both parties don't mention it at all. The minute one person doesn't mention a point on the answer choice, it's immediately wrong. Also, wrong answers focus on subjects or topics not mentioned in either argument.

Flaw Questions

Keywords: *error in reasoning, vulnerable to criticism, flaw, is not sound*

Summary: Argument. There's no hope in saving the conclusion and evidence. Ask how the conclusion does not necessarily follow 100%. Either the author overlooked a possibility (conclusion on steroids) or failed to assume something (evidence and conclusion not relevant). So ask, "What is the alternative possibility or assumption the author is not considering?" Next, match the flaw pattern (see Appendix D). Look at the conclusion, then the evidence. Are the two ideas unrelated? If so, you have an assumption problem. If both terms related but the conclusion is extreme, the author is overlooking a possible scenario. Now, describe the flawed gap (i.e., predict it).

There are a fixed number of patterns: confuses sufficient for necessary (e.g., X doesn't work in the evidence, so no Y [thinking X is needed and overlooking other possibilities]), numbers and percentages (50 people to 100 people from 1990

THE TRICKS OF THE TRADE IN LOGICAL-REASONING QUESTIONS

to 2000 do X, so a greater percentage of those people do X); uses a term in two different ways (equivocation); correlation in evidence so causation in conclusion; a part working in evidence so entire widget works in conclusion; some X bad in evidence, therefore all Y (too broad); X in evidence because not Y (circular reasoning; no other reason); theory one missing X in evidence so it must be the second theory that is correct (provides no proof for second theory); nutritionist claims in evidence because psychologist agrees in conclusion (wrong authority); only 1000 of X reported in evidence so must be Y (overlooks alternative possibility); because we don't know of X in evidence means X isn't true (overlooks possibility that X is actually true).

After making your prediction, go to the answer choices and see if each answer choice actually describes the argument in the right way (In other words, does it actually overlook a possibility or not make an assumption?) and then describes the correct flaw. For example, if the answer choice says that the argument overlooks a possibility but it does not, then that answer choice is immediately wrong.

Wrong Answer Choices: Will put the incorrect flaw (e.g., sufficient versus necessary) but the argument is really doing something else (e.g., generalizing from part to whole). No new piece of information can be introduced in an argument, as it can in strengthen/weaken question. When you identify the wrong flaw ask what the answer choice would need to look like for this flaw to be correct to really internalize the flaw pattern.

Common wrong-answer-choice traps are circular

reasoning (i.e., simply restating the conclusion without any evidence) and equivocation (using a word in two different ways). Also, test-makers will have an answer choice that focuses on solely the conclusion or the evidence, as opposed to the relationship between them, to trap you. Finally, test-makers love to say something accurate (e.g., it overlooks a possibility) but will not be the reason why the argument is flawed (i.e., why this particular evidence does not support this particular conclusion in the stimulus).

Parallel Flaw

Keywords: *error in reasoning similar, parallel, similarly vulnerable to criticism, flaw most similar*

Summary: Argument. There's no hope in saving the conclusion and evidence. Ask how the conclusion does not necessarily follow 100%. Then match this exactly to the answer choices. Start bottom-up from answer choice "E." Match flaw patterns. Put it in the abstract: A → B; B → C; therefore C → A (flaw). Then match precisely. If the stimulus confuses correlation for causation, then the correct answer choice must do the same. The answer choice can be out of order but, as long as the flaw is the same, it doesn't matter where the conclusion is stated.

Therefore, rearrange the premises so you have premises on top leading to the conclusion. Repeat the same for each answer choice and then compare to see if you have a parallel flaw. It's matching flaws, not matching words. Second, zoom into the conclusion and look at the modifiers. If stimulus has *will* in conclusion the parallel flaw must have *will* as well. If the stimulus has a qualifier such as *likely*, then, again, the correct answer choice cannot use a definite word such as *will*; it must have *likely* as well.

Wrong Answer Choices: Will be non-flawed arguments (i.e., valid arguments), or have the wrong modifier in the conclusion (*may* versus *will*, for example). Be careful of word play by the test makers. For example, if the conclusion is a prediction in a negative way (e.g., therefore he will not do X), they may twist the words by embedding a negative word into a positive word, such as "will be unsuccessful doing X" via the "un-". Notice that both conclusions are negative predictions nevertheless.

Parallel Reasoning

Keywords: parallel to, similar to, pattern of reasoning similar to

Summary: Argument. You need to match the argument perfectly to the answer choice. If the conclusion has hedging language, such as *could* or *may*, the correct answer choice must also have that. Therefore, compare conclusions to each other first and eliminate any answer choices that are different. If the stimulus has *will*, *could*, or *likely*, each answer choice must have that certainty (versus "more than," for example).

If the conclusion is making a weak prediction by using a modifier such as *likely to happen* then the answer choice also needs to have a weak prediction. Structure is key. If the stimulus provides you with "if D some E," "if E then G," and therefore "if D some G," the parallel argument must match exactly. You are trying to parallel the form of the argument, not the substance of it. Many parallel-reasoning questions use formal logic because it's easy to parallel. Next, compare evidences if you can't eliminate

Wrong Answer Choices: These will introduce too many variables. For example, if two people are mentioned in the stimulus, the wrong answer will introduce three people or items. Also, if the parallel argument has the same subject matter as the stimulus, it's most likely a trap answer and wrong. Finally, if the stimulus is using all categorical statements, the answer choice will throw particular statements, such as *some*, into the mix.

Principle (Rule on Top)

Keywords: *best illustrates the principle, most closely conforms to the principle, proposition, generalization, rule that justifies one of the judgments below*

Summary: Argument. This is all about applying the rule to the answer choices. A principle is a conditional statement (e.g., If P → Q). Your job is to look at the answer choices and find a scenario wherein when you hit the sufficient condition "P," and then "Q" follows. For example, if the general rule says, "if you're drunk and high then you're going to jail" (on top in the stimulus), your job is to find a scenario that matches this rule in the answer choices below. If the answer choice says "John was drunk; therefore he is going to jail," that would be wrong. You would need both conditions to trigger his going to jail.

Wrong Answer Choices: These will mention the incorrect example or fail a condition or be out of scope (i.e., bring in something not mentioned in stimulus). Also, if the rule concludes that therefore C must happen, a trap answer will say, "

C didn't happen because . . ." Basically, it will negate the rule. You cannot meet both conditions (being drunk and being high) and not go to jail. That would be a trap answer choice.

Strengthen Questions

Keywords: strengthen, answer choice most strongly supports

Summary: Argument. It's all about finding the assumption (relevant or on steroids?). Then strengthen it by shining a light on it; if the assumption is formal logic (if A, then B), find something to trigger A. This can also be done by finding an alternative possibility (a new piece of information) that can weaken the assumption and negating it by putting a "not" in front of it. Alternatively, if it's a common causal argument, putting a "not" in front of an alternative possibility can help strengthen it by saying that there is no other way other than "A causing B." A common pattern that you will see is a phenomenon in the evidence and a hypothesis or explanation for it in the conclusion.

By focusing solely on the assumption, you're making the conclusion more likely to follow from the evidence (not proving it 100%). When arguments lay out the benefits/drawbacks of A and benefits/drawbacks of B and then the conclusion chooses A, you want an answer choice that further strengthens A or further weakens B to "strengthen" the argument in favor of A.

Here answers with qualifiers such as *most* (as opposed to *some*) bolstering the assumption are great (unlike with inference questions), as you want the most powerful strengthening answer choice. Note: if the argument is lengthy, draw out a

T-chart to keep track of the pros and cons of each side. For example, say the crime rate is down by 20 percent because of a new police data widget. This assumes that nothing else caused the crime rate to drop and to strengthen it you just have to stymie another possibility from occurring (i.e., say that nothing else was the answer other than the widget).

Wrong Answer Choices: These will weaken the argument or be irrelevant to it. For example, if the argument is talking about smokers, a wrong answer choice will talk about non-smokers. Another common pattern is the stimulus is talking about water use in modern times and answer choice mentions water use in prehistoric times; it's irrelevant.

Weaken Questions

Keywords: most weakens, casts doubt, undermines

Summary: Argument. These are also all about finding the assumption (relevant or on steroids?). Then find an alternative to show it's not the only possibility so you can weaken the support between premise and conclusion. By focusing solely on the assumption, you're making the conclusion less likely to follow from the evidence (not disproving it 100%). Here answers with qualifiers such as *most* (as opposed to *some*) going against the assumption are great (unlike with inference questions), as you want the most powerful weaken answer choice. Note: if the argument is lengthy, draw out a T-chart to keep track of the pros and cons of each side.

A common pattern that you will see is a phenomenon in the evidence and an explanation for it in the conclusion. For example, let's say, again, that the crime rate down by 20 percent because of a new police data widget. This assumes that nothing else caused the crime rate to drop and to weaken, you just have to introduce another possibility.

Wrong Answer Choices: Trap answer choices will strengthen the argument, restate a fact from the stimulus, negate a premise, negate a conclusion, or will be irrelevant (i.e., will produce a "So what?" or "Who cares?" response). You can never attack the premise (it's always true) or solely attack the conclusion. It's all about weakening the support (i.e., the assumption), not the premise or conclusion. These two are the biggest traps testmakers employ.

Evaluate Questions

Keywords: evaluate, most useful in evaluating the argument

Summary: Argument. These are very rare on the LSAT; maybe you'll see one or two on each test. What are you dying to know? The correct answer choice needs to either strengthen or weaken the assumptions to an extreme in either direction. If asked to *evaluate except,* look for an irrelevant (out of scope) answer choice, something that doesn't have an impact on the argument.

Wrong Answer Choices: These are irrelevant; they have no bearing on the argument. Any answer choice that focuses in on isolating the conclusion or evidence alone, without the assumption, is wrong.

Sufficient Assumption

Keywords: if assumed

Summary: Argument. You need a very powerful assumption

to make the conclusion follow from the premise. The argument is missing a piece of the argument (one of the answer choices). For example: If A then B. Therefore B. The assumption is A. You have a premise on top, and a conclusion on the bottom, and your job is to supply the middle. This pattern is very common. Just plug the answer choice into the argument and fill the hole. These are very structurally friendly and relatively easy questions.

Think about categorical statements for this question type, valid arguments, and the "U" and reverse "U" assumption patterns. Remember: to be valid means 100% perfect. You need 100% powerful perfect support to make the conclusion necessarily follow from the evidence. Therefore, search for categorical and extreme language, such as *all* or *none*. The assumption will most likely not be related. Identify what's disconnected and find an answer choice that proves it beyond a doubt. For example, $100 is more than enough for a $6.00 Red Bull. No doubts, no questions.

Wrong Answer Choices: These will feature soft language, such as *at least* or *some*, and introduce a necessary assumption as the answer choice or just restate a piece of evidence. Also, they will put the conclusion of the argument (e.g., Y) as the sufficiency clause (after the *if* in the answer choice), but you cannot do that, as it confuses necessary for sufficient.

Necessary Assumption

Keywords: *assumed, argument depends, presupposes*

Summary: Argument. Think need. Ask, "Does the author need this for the conclusion to be valid?" Without the

THE TRICKS OF THE TRADE IN LOGICAL-REASONING QUESTIONS

assumption in the answer choice, the argument (the evidence leading to the conclusion) falls apart. Remember the Red Bull example from chapter two? Without $3.00 you cannot buy the Red Bull (it's necessary). Also think weak. You need a soft assumption to make the conclusion follow, such as *some*, *at least*, or *a few* (i.e., you just need to make the argument valid—not almighty powerful).

Necessary assumptions could be both: not related or on steroids. Lean towards thinking about an argument being on steroids and the argument overlooking a possibility. When you find the answer choice, deny it by negating it: "If X isn't true, does my argument fall apart?" If the answer is "yes," then you found the correct answer. Remember: the logical opposite of *some* is *none* and that of *all* is *not all* (i.e., some are not). On a harder necessary-assumption question, look for an answer choices that has *a not* in it, so if you deny it the argument falls apart.

Wrong Answer Choices: These will feature strong, powerful, extreme language such as *all*, *most*, or *none*. Any sufficient assumptions, or restatements of the evidence in stimulus, are wrong.

Now you have the tricks of the trade for both argument and non-argument logical-reasoning question types. The best way to see improvements in accuracy is to do the question types back to back. For example, do 10 main-point questions in a row (untimed). If you got the question wrong, identify why you chose an answer trap. What exactly led you to believe that the wrong answer was correct? Also, if you got the question correct, make sure you know why. If you guessed after narrowing it down to two possibilities then you did not fully understand the theory. Remember: there is only one correct answer and four incorrect answers. Now, let's take a break from arguments and touch upon my favorite section in the test: reading comprehension (RC).

8

READING COMPREHENSION: RESEARCHING, NOT READING

Reading comprehension, or "reading comp," is my favorite section. Yes, it's often boring and dense, but what do you think law school is going to be like? Not every case is going to be an exciting triple-homicide defense that you have to break down. A majority of the passages from this section come from journal articles that no one reads other than academic professors.

Therefore, the first thing you shouldn't be doing is just reading the passage from top to bottom and expecting to understand it. Whoever says that reading comprehension is nothing more than this is selling you "smoke and mirrors." Instead of reading, you will be researching. You will quickly figure out what the passage is about and why the author wrote it, and make notes to which you will want to refer back and start researching.

To excel at reading comprehension, you need to think in terms of evidence and conclusion versus just reading and trying to memorize. Various people will display this (author, critic, researcher, etc.) in the passage. Each person is making an argument and is supporting it with facts. For example, a scientist has a main point supported by evidence. Another scientist has a different conclusion supported by different evidence.

The author then determines which one to side with and why (i.e., presents his or her own argument) or simply just explains the two opposing viewpoints (i.e., doesn't pick a favorite). Thus, each reading comp passage will be either arguing something or providing information. Think about both scientists as opposing counsel arguing their case in front of a judge; the judge is the author and you are the jury watching the show and analyzing all the arguments.

So, in order to become attuned to the evidence-and-conclusion structure, you need to do several things. First, you have to really want to read the passage. Even if you don't care about fractal geometry or the theory of gravitation, for example, you have to act like you love it. On the test you will see four types of passages: law, humanities, natural science (hard science), and social science (soft science). All will be around 450-550 words, with five to eight questions. Sounds easy, but once you start reading, you will quickly find out that it gets hard fast.

Why? Here's what the test-makers do. They start with someone talking, usually the author, about someone else (e.g., a scientist). Then they throw some definitions around, add the viewpoints of some critics who don't believe in the scientist's theory, and then discuss another theory of, let's say, a second person is mentioned. Finally, they will make a claim about the scientist's hypothesis but ask you what the author thought about this claim. Okay, but the author didn't really have an opinion; he or she was just providing information. As you see, it gets complicated fast and has a lot of twists and turns.

The Purpose: Explain or Argue

Don't worry; here is how to master reading comprehension. First, understand the purpose of any passage you read. It's going to do two things for you: it will either provide you with information (*describe, explain, evaluate* something) or argue for something. I like the arguing passages because you can quickly find the author's opinion (conclusion) and support for it (evidence). So on the top of my reading comp section, before my eyes gloss over the first word, I write "Explain/Argue?" This way, in the back of my mind, I'm always thinking about the purpose.

How to Scan Keywords

It's very easy to get "lost in the sauce," or details. In fact, the biggest way in which I gained significant points on the reading comprehension was not by reading. I would literally run my eyes really fast over any hard-core details defined as definitions, examples to make a point clear, or research study results. Then I would find the comma (,) before or after the hard-core details to see what the point of it was and underline it.

The reason why you don't read the boring details is because two or three questions will ask you about them, so you will naturally have to go back anyway to read them. This can easily shave off two or three minutes by not rereading. Details are like a treasure hunt. Key nuggets are buried and you need to leave a trail to know where to go back and look. Therefore, if you see any hard-core details, make a note to the side, such as "DF" for definitions or "1/2/3" where the author is listing steps as evidence to support his or her main point. This way, you know that that is where you need to start your research after you read a detail question.

When I first attempted a passage I read every word, tried to understand what the facts were, and then went on to the questions. By the time I got to the questions I forgot what I had read; I had to go back and reread, and now my eight-minute passage (see Appendix F) turned out to be 12 minutes. Now I'm skipping over the details, thinking about the big picture and moving on fast.

The Most Important Question to Ask: Why?
Okay, the next way to master the reading-comp section is to ask, "Why did the author take time to sit down and write this?" This is the most important question I want you to ask yourself for every paragraph. This applies to the entire passage and to each individual paragraph. For example, once I'm done reading the first paragraph I'll take a deep breath, pause, and think purpose. So, I'll simply ask, "Why?" and then jot it down.

Is the author making his main point in paragraph one? Is he introducing a topic or stating the critic's viewpoint? Is the author providing support for his main point or support for why he disagrees with a critic? Whatever it is, jot it down in no more than three or four words (e.g. "support" or "Author Main Point"). Never regurgitate verbatim from the passage. You need to own the material and the only way to do that is to put it in your own words. If there are four paragraphs in the passage, pause after each paragraph and ask "Why?" Drill this question into your head and I promise you it will pay dividends.

The Push-Up Method

Now, once you identify the main point of the passage, ask yourself, "How does each paragraph relate to this?" This is what I call the "push-up method." How does this sentence or paragraph link up with the main point? So, if the main point is stated in paragraph one, I'll underline this and then for every subsequent paragraph I'll ask, "What does this paragraph have to do with the main point?" Oh, it gives an example of the author's main point, or it gives a counter-example to the critic's viewpoint, so the author disagrees—got it. This will let you take the big picture out of the passage in usually about two or three questions from each section; that's an easy 8-12 points you can bag by simply asking "Why?"

How to Take Notes

Should you take notes? Yes. But don't underline everything. Underline the main point and circle the examples. After each paragraph, stop and underline any strong opinion words, adjectives, adverbs, recommendations, or extreme words you see. For example: *lovely, clearly, must, should, never, none*, etc. The critical piece, however, is to underline after you read the paragraph, not while you're reading it. This ensures that you will be forced to think about structure (i.e., conclusion and evidence) instead of just hunting for the words right there on the spot.

Usually there will be something important (conclusion) followed by tons of examples (evidence) illustrating that point. After these keywords, the author or critic or whoever's view is presented will provide examples indicated by *for example, for instance*, a colon (:), etc. Usually, whatever is before or after these evidence indicators are the main points of the paragraph; circle these keywords.

How to Predict
Alternatively, to find the main point, look for the examples and ask, "What is this an example of and why did the author include this?" This will serve as the main point. Then, before moving on to the next paragraph, predict what is going to happen next, just like in a mystery movie. Anticipation is key. If you're wrong, even better, as it will enable you to be more curious and see where the next passage is heading. This really enables the reading-comp reasoning structure to stick and prevents you from rereading.

Don't Do the Questions in Order
Next is tackling the questions; the secret not doing them in order. First, look for the big-picture questions such as "The main point, primary purpose of the passage is?" After that,

scan for the detail questions that require you to research: any question that has a keyword that makes you go back to the passage and start digging for the answer, such as *according to the passage* or *based on the passage*. Finally, seek the inference questions: any questions that start with "the passage provides the most support" or "the author would most likely agree with" or any question with the word "infer."

Remember that inferences must be true and there must be a specific line item from the passage (e.g., line 55) that you can support your answer with. Finding inferences is a fact-finding skill that requires you to combine duplicate terms and make contrapositives. So, if the answer choice has "all X" but paragraph three says "some X or all Y," you know it's wrong. I also noticed that the exact word is duplicated in the correct answer choice with that of the line item to the passage. If you are unsure about an answer choice say, "Did the author say XYZ?" Then go find the word or words specifically in the paragraph. If you can put your finger on the sentence then you can't go wrong.

Also, just like in logical-reasoning inference questions, any answer choice that is extreme (i.e., has *most, all, every, none*, etc.) is usually wrong, unless it's supported by that passage. Therefore, if you have 30 seconds left, scan for the extreme words and quickly eliminate answer choices to increase your chance of guessing correctly.

Basic detail questions, on the other hand, will test your ability to deliver back a summary of the details. Any paragraph that has tons of definitions, examples, or lists, are prime for details. Test-makers love to actually use "detail except" questions such as "All of the following were mentioned in the passage except?" Since detail questions are generally easier than inference questions, they make it more time-consuming by making you go through the process of elimination; you have to go back to the passage and eliminate the wrong answers to find the correct one. It's like an acceptability question in logic games, where the rules break four out of five answers and your job is to find the one answer choice that the rule didn't break.

Reading Comprehension Question Strategy

Big Picture (easy 8-12 points)
↓
Detail (with key words)
↓
Inference (with key words)

The Three-Minute Rule

To master timing, read the passage and don't spend more than three minutes on it. Since you have approximately eight minutes per passage, this will leave you about six minutes to attack the big picture, detail, and inference questions. In the beginning you will notice that the hardest part with reading comp is timing. With more passages under your belt it will get easier, as you will start to see patterns and get better at understanding the passages (see Appendix G).

Everything you need is found in the passage. So don't worry about or care about the story or facts. Think about evidence/conclusion for each party to the case, why the author wrote the passage (to provide info or argue something), and why the author brought in each paragraph, and then knock out the questions from big picture to keyword detail to inference. If a question doesn't have a keyword that lets you quickly go back to the paragraph to find what you need to research, then it's going to be very time-consuming. Thus, if you are short on time, skip these.

Finally, remember that any answer choice not supported specifically by the passage (e.g., a misquote; something that is irrelevant, like talking about non-smokers versus smokers; or extreme language, such as using *all* instead of *some*) is incorrect. In other words, the biggest mistake you can make is relying on your memory. So many trap answers are designed specifically for this.

Mastering the Comparative Passage
As far as the comparative passage, where there are two mini-passages versus one long passage, you are doing exactly the same thing as above. Just note that the topic for each one will be the same but the purposes will be different. Before you do the comparative passage, quickly glance at the question sets to see if there are more questions talking about passage B than question A, for example, and if so, read that passage first and knock out the big picture, detail, and inference questions for that one first. The Ω important thing to remember is that you are seeing how both passages are alike and different. Keep that in the back of your mind and you'll be able to get through it with accuracy.

Finally, if you get an answer choice narrowed down to two choices (e.g., B or C) don't "spin your wheels" thinking; move to another question and then come back to it before you leave the passage. The minute I started taking these action steps I achieved clarity as to the correct answer choice and saved up to two minutes on my timing. This is critical; however, you must practice it so it becomes second nature.

9

PRACTICE MAKES ALMOST PERFECT

Prepping for the LSAT is an emotional rollercoaster. There will be days when you want to cry and give up and there will be times (when you least expect it) when everything just clicks: the ultimate, euphoric "a-ha" moment. The only way to overcome the highs and lows is to ride out the volatility, as they say in the stock market; it's to stay in it for the long haul and not give up; the way you do that is practice, practice, practice. Here is what practice doesn't mean: taking full-length practice tests for a month back to back until the test day. That's like shooting free throws for a month and expecting all your shots to fall in every professional game.

You must first learn the proper form for how to shoot the ball so the ball falls in. Likewise, you must fully understand the logical principles in the logical-reasoning section (i.e., finding out if the conclusion necessarily follows or probably follows from the evidence), finding what Could Be True, Must Be False, and Must Be True in logic games, and finding the main point and reading for structure in the reading-comprehension section. Master the basics; then do timed sections.

The Six-Month Study Plan

Think of the LSAT as five 35-minute sections with a 10-15 minute break in between, as opposed to a three- to four-hour test. The best strategy to do this is over the course of six months, with four hours a day, Monday through Saturday. If you don't have six months, break up the schedule accordingly, but keep the themes the same (e.g., doing logical reasoning with another section on any given day).

The First Three Months

For the first three months, internalize the material, do untimed practice questions, and review answers from each section. Every time you do logical-reasoning study sessions, alternate them with logic games or reading comp. For example, two hours in the morning of logical reasoning and two hours in the afternoon of logic games or reading comprehension. Alternatively, if you like to knock it all out at once, do one sitting for four hours with a 30-minute break in between the sections.

The Fourth and Fifth Months

Next, for the fourth and fifth months, focus solely on timing by letting the timer run as you do the alternating sections and jotting down which problem types (flaw, inference, etc.) trip you up. This is how you realize which problem type takes you the longest, so you can make smart choices within a fraction of a second when you see it on game day. The LSAT test-makers want to know how many steps it takes to knock you off the "LSAT game." For example, if they throw a very difficult question (e.g., question four) in the logical-reasoning section, will you spend three or four minutes trying to solve it or will you choose not to do it?

If you are adamant about solving it, then you have traded off two or three potentially easier questions that require less time (e.g., one minute and 30 seconds each), which means two or three fewer points at the cost of one point in the same amount of time. Thus, by timing every section throughout months four and five, you will master exactly which problems to skip and which ones to do on test day. Like conditioning for a marathon, a UFC fight, or a boxing event, your goal is to make your pencil strokes automatic.

If someone throws a left jab at you, your body should move to the right. If you sense you lost 45 seconds on an LSAT question, you should move on. Only by being relentless with your timing will you condition your body to automatically do things in high-stress environments. This way, you're just worrying about solving the problem versus solving the problem and worrying about timing. Thus, timing is of the essence—especially on test day.

Time more than questions; time everything. Time the minutes it takes you to wake up, get in your car, get your coffee, drive to the library, and sit down and start working out your brain. I saw massive improvements in my score when I realized what my time was worth per question, per minute, and per hour. I want you to have timing engrained into your blood. After all, that is the lifeline of an attorney's livelihood—billable hours, right?

The Sixth Month

Finally, month six is all about making sure you hit your accuracy goals within the time limitations. If you're shooting for a 160, you know that you need 20 correct out of 25 or 26, so you have five or six to skip. Knowing which ones to quickly skip and guessing the minute you see them (e.g., on a formal-logic or principle question) will ensure you hit your targeted score.

Also, make sure on Saturday morning (or Monday if the real test falls on that day) to take the full five-section practice test (not four sections). You can throw in a random section from an Prep Test (any test from 1-40) so you can keep newer prep tests fresh as you get closer to test day since that will more likely mimic the LSAT "style" of questions. For example, the prep tests in the 20's series tested heavily on flaws whereas the newest prep tests from the 70's series focused heavily on logical reasoning principle questions.

If you use a section from a 70's test you will run out of fresh material later when you need it the most. By the time you take your real test you should have done at least 20 full-length, five-section, 35-minute practice tests—approximately 60 hours of simulated intensive prep-testing. Not to mention the 480 hours of studying. How badly do you want it? It's not going to get any easier in law school when you are doing eight hours a day in the library, or in court when you're prepping for a big case. So you might as well start conditioning your body and mind now.

An important thing to remember is that this test is not about doing all 77 Prep Tests because all that does is build endurance, and without strategy and understanding the fundamentals, you will not see results. That's like saying "I want to weigh 110 pounds within 90 days," but every day you eat the same foods and then step on the scale in the morning and see no results. It's like running on a treadmill; you're going nowhere fast. Also, don't do problem after problem without correcting your mistakes.

Thoroughly review your answers and know why you picked the right one and what tripped you up to pick the wrong one and jot it down. There is only one correct answer; each of the other choices has a word that makes it wrong. Review every problem, not just the ones you got wrong. This is crucial.

Timing Strategy

Finally, one great way to make sure you have mastered the material and timing (i.e., to measure results) is to do a timed section and redo the same one a week or two later. When you do it the first time, identify which ones you missed and circle the correct answer. Then put that section away (in a drawer so you won't be tempted to peek at it) and redo it by printing out a fresh new copy. I saw serious improvements when I discovered this strategy.

Now analyze the results. Did you pick the same answer as the first time? If you did, that means you need to go back into the study phase and learn how to do that question type again. If you improved, did you do so by luck or did you know what tripped you up in the first place? Did you do worse? If so, maybe you spent too much time on another question that slowed you down.

Doing repeat exercises will give you a tremendous advantage when you take the real test. Although practice doesn't ensure a perfect score, it will increase the likelihood of you achieving your targeted score. Thus, practice makes almost perfect.

10

PLAYING GAMES (ANALYTICAL REASONING)

The analytical-reasoning or "logic games" section is all about reading rules, making deductions (inferences) from them, and then answering questions regarding what Must Be True, Cannot Be True (MBF), or Could Be True. It's about seeing all possible options and then determining, based on the question asked, which option the question applies to. In other words, find the truth from all possibilities.

Multiple Sketches
In fact, the key to increasing accuracy and timing in each type of logic game is creating multiple possibilities or sketches from the beginning; the more sketches or "what if" worlds you can create, the better you will become at succeeding in

this section. For example, if a rule places a variable, H, in two different positions (say, the first and second out of five slots), then once you draw out these two options (i.e., put H in slot 1 and H in slot 2 and fit the other variables in place from the other rules), you can determine what Must Be True, Could Be True, and Cannot Be True (MBF). For a Must Be True correct answer, H must work in any given option or scenario. For a Could Be True correct answer, H must work in at least one possible option. For a Cannot Be True (MBF), H cannot work in any of the options.

Think about it: if you figure out all the possibilities up front before moving on to the questions, then there isn't a question you cannot answer. Conversely, if you just draw the initial, or "master," sketch, and then rush to the questions, the test-maker is going to ask you maybe one or two (out of five to seven questions) on the basic sketch but then will test to see if you have taken the time to consider the second or third "what-if "world. Thus, it behooves you to take the time to draw multiple sketches from the beginning.

Once you master finding out what must be true or false from all possibilities, you will crush the games section. In order to master these skills you need practice, practice, and more practice. It's like playing a new sport. Once you get the proper form down, it's just practicing every day until you become great. For example, the first time I learned how to lift weights, I had no idea how to put my fingers on the curl bar or chest bar, how many reps or sets to do, how to breathe, etc. After months of working out and lifting weights it became instinct; it's the same with logic games. Do a logic game every day and redo it until you get the timing down to under eight minutes; you will memorize the deductions and it will become instinct to you. Time is the answer.

Thus, I would again argue that logic games are the easiest section in which you can see massive improvements in your score, because all the games are clones of each other. There are only so many ordering and grouping games that can be put into place; there are only a finite amount of iterations without rules and master sketches overlapping. Therefore, a great strategy is doing back-to-back games by type (see Appendix E).

Logic Games are Fun
Once you start the games and get the hang of them you will love them; they are fun. I remember that when I got really good was after I forced myself to do one game every morning when I got up. It got me in the habit of switching gears to "LSAT mode" and after a quick subsequent review, I started internalizing the deductions and it became second nature to me.

The best thing about the games is that after you make your initial sketch and make the deductions, every variable fits nicely into the questions, just like a jigsaw puzzle. Unlike the other sections, where you may have it boiled down to two answer choices, in logic games you will quickly see that you either have the perfect match or no match (which means that you drew your sketch incorrectly or you missed a key deduction). It's like solving an equation: there is only one right answer.

The Fantastic Four

Every game asks you to do something. In general, you will be asked to put items in order or into groups. Sometimes you may be asked to match two sets of entities together as well. Basically, there are four actual actions that you can take on test day: order, distribute/select, match, and group. Also, you may do both together in a game known as a "hybrid game." Overall, you're asked to put people in order from tallest to shortest, put people into teams for a game, match color combinations to cars, etc. Also, some games have single entities and some have multiple entities:

Logic-Games "Fantastic Four":

1. Ordering (strict or loose) . . . . single entity
2. Grouping I (selection or choosing) . . . . . . single entity
3. Grouping II (distribute, accompany) . more than one entity
4. Matching . . . . more than one entity

ORDERING GAMES (KEYWORDS: SEQUENCING, ORDERING, SCHEDULING, RANKING):

Ordering games can involve both strict and loose ordering. With strict ordering, the variables are put into fixed slots (e.g., A comes immediately before B). With loose ordering, the variables are put in relation to each other (e.g., A comes before B). Notice how, unlike strict ordering, loose ordering doesn't tell you how much earlier A comes (it could come one position earlier or 10 positions earlier).

You will want to ask the following questions when going through the rules to bag all the deductions: Who can be first? Who can be last? Who can't be first? Who can't be last? Who has no relationship to the others (i.e., who is the "floater" who can go anywhere in the sketch)? Which variables can you combine? Many of these questions are asking if you can see a variable that is in front of a chain that can also occupy the back of a chain, or vice versa. Typical sketches for both strict and loose ordering include the strict hangman sketch and the spider-web sketch:

Hangman and Spider-Web Sketches

Strict Hangman: (ABCDEFG)   Loose Spider Web: (ABCDEFG)

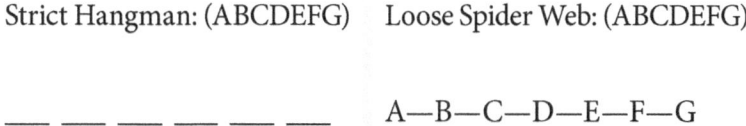

Making deductions or inferences will come from combining rules to form blocks. For example, if a rule says, "A comes immediately before B," you know that B can never go first because A has to come before it. Also, A can never go last because B has to come after it. Now if there are only five slots and a rule states, "B cannot be last," then you know that this "AB" block can only be in slots one and two, two and three, or three and four. So now you have three possible scenarios and you can immediately draw out three sub sketches to capture all the possibilities. Then you can figure out what Cannot Be True (MBF) (0), Could Be True (1-100), and Must Be True (100) for each and every sketch based on the rules that discuss the placement of the other variables (CDEFG). The most possibilities, or scenarios that you will see per rule are three, which is uncommon; two possibilities is customary, as the test-makers know that you are under time constraints.

Option 1: Strict Hangman: (ABCDEFG)

___ ___ ___ ___ ___ ___

  A B

Option 2: Strict Hangman: (ABCDEFG)

___ ___ ___ ___ ___ ___

     A B

Option 3: Strict Hangman: (ABCDEFG)

___ ___ ___ ___ ___ ___

         A B

Now, on a Could Be True question, any option (i.e., any of the sketches above) works for the question. If you see an answer choice that has AB in slots one and two in your first sketch and in slots three and four in your second sketch, then the answer to the question "Can B, be placed in slot four?" is yes, because it has to be true in just one possibility or world (sketch three). Conversely, on a Must Be True question, the right answer must display correctly in all possibilities.

For loose ordering, similar rules apply. However, instead of being fixed into slots, the rules will give you relative positions. For example: A comes before B and D comes before A.

PLAYING GAMES (ANALYTICAL REASONING)

Your job is to link the rules together and determine who can be first, who can be last, who cannot be first, and who cannot be last. I like to circle the entities that can be first and box the entities that can be last. So if a question asks, "Who can be first?" you know it must be "D" because it precedes both A and B. Likewise, if the question asks you "What must be false?" you know that "B" can never be first or second because it has two people in front of it; therefore, it must be third.

On a real LSAT problem the test-makers will present several variables that could make your linking chain confusing. When you get stuck on a question, always ask yourself "How many people in front of X?" and "How many people behind X?" This way, you know exactly where variable X can go and cannot go. Thus, when in doubt, count to get back on track.

Link-up Rules Example: D—A—B

GROUPING I GAMES (SELECTING, CHOOSING):

Grouping I games involve taking a larger group of people and breaking them up into smaller groups. You will be selecting who's going to be in and who's going to be out. You also will be selecting some people and rejecting others. The reason why it's "grouping I," as opposed to "grouping II," is that there is only one set of variables. In grouping II games, you will be doing basically the same thing with two sets of variables broken down into more groups.

Grouping I games are going to test your formal-logic

skill set (if-then statements). Most importantly, they will test whether you can keep track of who's selected and who's not selected. This is all about the "or" and "not both" rules mentioned in chapter two. The key in these games is to make multiple sketches when you learn of a rule concerning who can or cannot go into a group. For example, let's say that if Robert is selected, then Mary and David are not selected.

Draw two sketches and create both worlds to see what the possibilities are. Also, and most importantly, think of what the minimum and maximum number can possibly be for the members of the group who are in and members of the group who are out. To help keep track of the members, make sure to contrapose the rules after you write them out and combine the middle terms to make inferences. For example:

Rule 1 says: If A—**B**

Rule 2 says: IF **B**—**C**

Rule 3 says: IF **C**—D

Here you can conclude that A is enough to guarantee us B, C, and D. These are the key types of inferences that you will be tested on in grouping games. If you are ever stuck combining the rules, then make sure that you have formed the contrapositive of them, as that will most likely give you the missing piece to enable you to combine them. Now, the key questions you want to ask when going through the rules are: Does everyone have to be in groups? Can any groups be empty? Can entities repeat in groups? How many entities to spots are there? Are there any unfilled spots in the groups? A simple sketch for this would look something like a T-chart:

Larger Group (ABCDEFG)

In   Out

The "Or" Rule

A rule in a grouping game will often have an "or" in it, indicating that either one entity or the other is in (maybe both). For example, let's say that, "X or Y is in group A," which means, "if not X, then Y is in," and the contrapositive: "if not Y, then X is in." This means that group A cannot be empty; at least one must be in (maybe both X and Y). Notice how you go from a negative (not X) to a positive (then Y) with the "or."

OR Rule: At Least One Always In (Maybe Both)

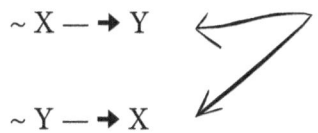

~X —→ Y

~Y —→ X

The "Not Both" Rule: Enemies

On the other hand, a rule can state the same as above with the qualifier "but not both." For example, let's say that either X or Y is in group A, but not both. Here you are going from a positive to a negative. This translates to: if X, then not Y; if Y, then not X (the contrapositive). Thus, the group is now reduced by one since X and Y are enemies (i.e., the maximum number that can be in this group is reduced by one and maybe no one is in the group). Basically, you can never have X and Y together.

Not Both Rule: At Least One Always Out (Maybe Both)

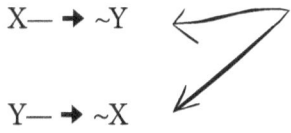

Enemies:

So, when a rule says, "P or T, but not both," write "never PT" or "either P/T" in that specific "out" group. Next, think about the numbers and the possibilities. Draw different sketches early on to see all possibilities and determine what must be true and false from what could be true and false. Draw "P" in the first group, then "P" in the second group, etc.

However, if there are more than two sketches that can be drawn (i.e., tons of possibilities), don't waste your time and jump into the questions. Also, after you write the rules, ask, "What's the flip side to it?" For example, if a rule says, "K can't be in group O" (and there's only one other group for it: W), then write down "K must be in W."

Usually selection games have tons of "what if" CBT/CBF questions, so this is a sign that you just have to move to the questions faster, as the inferences will come from the questions. On the other hand, when you have tons of MBT/MBF questions, you know that the majority of the inferences are coming from the various sketches done before moving on to the questions.

One final thing about grouping I games, going back to chapter two, when I discussed sufficient and necessary, is that when you don't trigger the sufficient condition (left side of the arrow), then the rule is irrelevant. For example, let's say that "If ~X, then Y" is the rule, but the question asks, "If X, then what happens?" Well, you don't know and therefore cannot conclude a Must Be True answer.

Likewise, if you just trigger the "Y," or the necessary condition, the rule is also irrelevant, as you avoided the sufficient trigger "~X". Finally, if you fail the necessary condition (i.e., say "not Y"), then you have to fail the sufficient condition (i.e., say that X is in); in other words, you're taking the contrapositive.

The In-and-Out Sketch

This is very useful in simple, fixed grouping games with, let's say, an "in" column and an "out" column. You draw a "T" chart and label your columns "in" and "out." Then you figure out what happens if X is in, if X is not in, if Y is in, if Y is not in, etc. Note: in a simple game with only an "in and out" option, if the variable is not in, then it's out and vice versa, since it's binary. Here's a simple illustration of a chained rule:

Example of rules combined: ~ X → Y → Z → ~W → P

IN	OUT
Y	X
Z	N
P	W

So, remember that everything on the left is sufficient and everything on the right is necessary. Now, let's assume that you have an "in/out" T-chart and the question asks you "If Y is out, what must be true?" Well, if you fail a necessary condition (i.e., not Y), then you have to take the contrapositive of it, meaning that X is now in. Since you had "If ~X, then Y," you're now saying ~Y (i.e., it's out), so therefore X has to be in.

IN	OUT
X (MBT)	Y

~ X — → ~ Y— → Z — → ~ W — → P

Now, you have failed the necessary condition "Y," which also served as the sufficient condition for Z because it was to the left side of the arrow in that chain. Therefore, when you fail the sufficient condition, the rule disappears and now "Z" doesn't have to be in the group; it could be either in or out (i.e., it's now a floater); floaters are usually wrong answer choices for MBT/MBF questions. So always look to the relationship between the chains and analyze the sufficient and necessary conditions. The test-makers will test you heavily on finding the truth for sufficient and necessary conditions.

GROUPING II GAMES (DISTRIBUTE, ACCOMPANY, FORM GROUPS WITH 2+ ENTITIES):

In grouping II games, you will have two (or more) sets of variables. Your task will be to do basically the same thing as in grouping I games, only with more groups (i.e., sub-groups) involved. Either it won't be a binary setup (in/out) or there will be multiple sub-categories. For example, distribute group one entities (ABCDE) into three groups (I, II, III). If you put together a pick-up basket ball game with 20 ballers on the sideline that can only fit into three teams (Team A, B, and C) of at least 5 players each, you just did a grouping II game.

The most important lesson here is figuring out what the maximum and minimum numbers of the various groups can be. So, if variables A and B go into group I, then you have three variables left (CDE) to spread over the two remaining groups (groups II and III). Or if five players go into team A and seven go into team B, which go into team C? Usually with these types of games, all players or variables are used up and there are no repeats (e.g., baller Curry can't play for both teams).

Also, grouping II, like grouping I, will test your ability to master the language of the "or" and "not both" rules. They will say that X and Y cannot be together (i.e., they are enemies) or sometimes together (i.e., at least one must be in at all times). You have to be able to quickly translate the possibilities once you see these rules (e.g., ~ XY block and always XY block). One set are enemies, and the other set are best friends forever (BFFs). Finally, the more concrete you can make your sketch, the better. If a rule says, "W cannot be in Team B," then physically put a " ~ W" underneath team B, which implies that it has to be in Team A or Team C. Always convert negative rules into positive ones.

The questions you want to ask in grouping II games are: How large and small can the groups be? Can any groups be empty? Remember that if a game doesn't specifically state whether entities can go into the group, you cannot assume that. Some harder games will have the possibility of a group being empty. The less fixed (i.e., more vague) the initial setup is, the harder the game will be. The rules are there for you to narrow all your possibilities down into a couple of options. However, after you go through all your rules and you can still draw five or six possibilities, then that's a good sign that a game will be significantly harder than the rest. A simple sketch for this would look like:

The Roster Sketch

ABCDEFGHIJKLMNO (ball players)

Team A	Team B	Team C
___	___	___
___	___	___
___	___	___
___	___	___
___	___	___
___	___	___
___	___	___

MATCHING GAMES (DISTRIBUTE, ACCOMPANY, FORM GROUPS):

Matching games involve matching two (or more) entity sets to each other, just as you match your clothes every morning—it's no different. Just like grouping II games, you will definitely have two or more variable sets, but the main difference is that the entities can repeat. For example, let's say that you have a basketball team of players (ABCDE) and you have to give each player a gift for winning the finals (Rolex, Lamborghini, oceanfront condo). Here, you're matching gifts to the players. Sometimes a player may get two gifts depending on how many scores he or she put up (it's stated in the rules).

Key questions to ask yourself in order to make deductions are: How many times can you use a variable? What are the minimum number of entities and maximum number of entities (gifts) each player can get? If the rule says, "variables can be used at least once," that means you can possibly use the variable indefinitely. For example, Curry gets at least one Rolex, but could get seven if the game permits.

A simple roster sketch would be used in a grouping II game:

ABCDE (ball players)

Rolex   Lamborghini   oceanfront condo

_____   _____   _____

_____   _____   _____

Alternatively, you can create a chart with your entities listed on top (ABCDE) and your gifts listed on the side (R/L/O), and can you check off who gets what and use an "X" when a player does not receive a certain item.

The Chart Sketch

	A	B	C	D	E
Rolex (R)	✓	X	✓	✓	✓
Lambo (L)	X	X	✓	X	X
Ocean Condo (O)	X	X	X	X	✓

HYBRID GAMES (COMBINATION OF ACTIONS):

In a hybrid game, you're doing two sets of actions at a time (e.g., ordering and matching). You could be ordering people and assigning attributes to them. For example, you could put the basketball players in order from those scoring the most points to those scoring the least and also assigning their toys (Rolex, Lambo, or condo). You could be ordering people and distributing them into smaller groups (as in grouping II games).

For example, you could put the players in order from the highest-scoring to the lowest-scoring and then form two smaller groups so they play one on one. You could also order two (or more) sets of entities simultaneously so you have layers of hangman sketches on top of each other. The more items you have to order, just keep stacking them on top of each other.

The Stack Sketch

__ __ __ __ __ __ (ABDCEFG)

__ __ __ __ __ __ (RSTUVW)

The more actions you have to go through, the more time-consuming the game will be, so hybrid games are good to skip over if you are short on time. The best strategy for this game is to make separate sketches. If you have to order, make an ordering sketch (strict or loose). If you have to match, then make a matching sketch. Next, when you see the rules, figure out which sketch it's referring to. That's about it. Although it seems frightening, it's not that bad. It is time-consuming, though. The questions you will want to ask yourself are: Which rules apply to which sketch? What are my maximum and minimum limitations? As far as your sketches go, just draw out both actions separately, as discussed earlier. Put them side by side, something like this:

ABCDE (ball players)

Rolex	Lamborghini	oceanfront condo
___	___	___
___	___	___

Loose: (ABCDEFG)

A—B—C—D—E—F—G

Mastering Rules and Deductions:
Once you learn what task or action you are supposed to take, go through the rules and restrictions and jot them down.

PLAYING GAMES (ANALYTICAL REASONING)

Next, start writing down all the variables on your paper (e.g., ABCDEF). Also, go through the rules and write them out in the language of formal logic (e.g., X → Y) as well, and make your master sketch. When you write out your rule write it out completely, as you will use your shorthand for this later on.

What I discovered is that when I read the opening paragraph I take my pencil and cross out each sentence after I sketch it or jot it down. This way, I don't miss an important word that can make my entire sketch wrong. For example, if it says "at least one" and you mistaken that for "one," your entire sketch will blow up and you may end up missing all the points in the game. Another common error I made was mistaking "immediately before" for "before" in ordering games. Eliminating errors is just a matter of practice. The more games you can do, the better you will become.

The great thing about logic games is that once your sketch, or setup, is correct, all the questions will fit in like the pieces of a puzzle. There can only be one true correct answer. Therefore, try to milk the game for whatever you can up front. Draw multiple options (sketches) early. Remember: that's taking a possible scenario and subdividing it into multiple scenarios to refine the game so it's easier—the more finite and concrete you can make things, the easier this section will become. This way, you will be prepared to answer what Must Be True, Must Be False, or Could Be True based on each sketch/option.

A Must Be True (MBT) answer must be consistent in all sketches, whereas a Could Be True (CBT) just needs to be correct in one of the possible sketches. Also, for Could Be True questions, lean towards testing "floaters," or entities not mentioned at all in a rule. Since no rule restricts them, they are "free birds" to go wherever you want in the sketch. Finally, a Must be False (MBF) cannot be true in any of the options.

Now take a step back and let the deductions hit you in the face. This is what pays big dividends and lets you bag points fast. One thing to think through is to see if any of the rules duplicate, or have an entity that's mentioned in both rules. To make deductions, combine rules (i.e., duplicates found in each rule) and/or contrapose, and then combine again (trace your way to 180.).

As long as you did your sketch and translated the rules correctly, you should be able to see what Must Be True, Cannot Be True (MBF), and Could Be True relatively quickly. Also, ask how many entities there are in relation to slots or groups. If you have five entities (players) and only three groups, then two entities will be left out (unless the rules say otherwise).

Sometimes the game will give you a "not both" rule, such as "if entity Curry plays for Team A, then he doesn't play for Team B." If the rules give you an opportunity to limit your options within the sketch, think about making two sketches and putting Curry in both of them to see what happens; these are, in essence, all of your possibilities in the universe of this game. Always exhaust all possibilities so you know exactly where everyone could, must, or cannot go in both sketches.

ATTACKING THE QUESTIONS

Rule-Eliminator Questions

Okay, now you're ready for the questions. For every question you attempt, go back to your shorthand sketch of the rules. The first question usually asks, "Which of the following is an acceptable order . . . ?" Take each rule to each answer choice and if the rule violates it completely, cross it out. These "rule-eliminator questions" are four easy points that you can bag, as they are almost always featured in each game (and there are four games in a section). On a side note, these rule eliminator questions allow you to see how the sketch should be set up, as they lay out the entities in order for you. So, if you're stuck in drawing your sketch, take a peek at the acceptability questions.

MBT Questions

Next, if you were able to make your deductions (i.e., combining rules and drawing various sketches to see all possibilities), try the Must Be True questions first. Remember from chapter two that anything that Could Be False or Must Be False is wrong. Do your Must Be False questions next. It's the same thing here—anything that Could Be True or Must Be True is wrong.

CBT Questions

Finally, do the "what if" questions. These will start with something like "If Curry plays for Team A, then which of the following could be true?" These can also ask what Must Be True. The good thing, if you were able to make various sketches and possibilities beforehand, is that you can refer to that specific sketch to answer the questions. Note: these "what if" questions are good to do if you couldn't make too many deductions up front.

Sometimes the game won't allow you to, or you may just not see them at first. Also, if you see any questions that substitute a rule and ask you to replace it with another rule, then run. It will eat up a lot of your time and chances are you may still get it wrong. It's not a good return on your time investment. Every LSAT question is worth one point, whether the question is easy, medium, or hard.

TIMING STRATEGIES FOR GAMES

Timing for games is also critical. What I found that really trips you up is not seeing a deduction. You might have three or four rules written out in shorthand, but then you don't see the duplication. In that scenario, don't just stare at the page; move immediately to the Could Be True or "if" questions. In other words, if you were able to make many deductions, do the Must Be True or Cannot Be True (MBF) questions first. Conversely, if you're five minutes into the game and don't see the deduction, then move to the "if" questions and start drawing that hypothetical "if H is in slot 3, then . . . ." to see how the other rules affect it. Every game will have two or three tough questions.

For me, it took a lot of discipline to skip these and move on to the next game. Never spend more than eight or nine minutes on a game: four minutes for the sketch and deductions and four or five minutes for the questions. If you're eight and half minutes in and answered three questions, guess on the remaining ones and move to the next game.

The worst thing you can do is attempt a hard question, narrow it down to two answer choices, burn three more minutes, and then get it wrong anyways. It's better to guess and come back if you have time. Good timing requires discipline and habit. When you are under stress, your subconscious takes over. Thus, train your body and mind to move naturally, so on test day it will be second nature.

Finally: practice, practice, practice. There are only so many variations you can see on this standardized test. The content will be different, but the rules will become familiar. Always figure out the game's action, see if there are one or two entities you have to work with, combine duplicates and contrapose the rules, sketch out the possible scenarios, and hit the questions hard from Must Be True to Could Be True (i.e., "if" questions). Get in and out in under nine minutes.

In the beginning, I was only be able to do two games within the time allowed, but after weeks of practicing I got good at knowing what not to do and thus got up to completing three games. This was exactly where I wanted to be to hit my score. If you're willing to put in the hard work and focus your energy on knowing exactly which problems will take up too much time and choosing not to do them, then you will see a big jump in points on the logic-games section of the LSAT.

11

PERFECT PRACTICE: SCRIPTS TO THINK

In business, to perfect a process you need to be able to measure it. In order to measure it, you need a reliable indicator. For me it was tried and tested sales scripts. If my sales agents called upon 300 clients, I wanted to ensure that they were all reading off the same page to know whether or not my script was working. Imagine deploying different questions and saying different things each time a sales call is made. How could you ever measure anything? The same goes for the LSAT.

In order for you to master the logical-reasoning and reading-comp sections, you need a series of questions repeated in your mind over and over again to get you to think about the right answer. Here is what I discovered that helped me really break through the periods when I felt I was hitting a wall. I recommend printing this out and having these questions in front of you every time you are doing a logical-reasoning or reading-comprehension passage.

Thinking About Games

Since the logic games each contain different tasks and rules, there is no general thinking script. However, for any game you attempt, think about the action (order, group, select, match, etc.), the entities (one variable set or two), and the deductions after duplicating common terms in the rules and contraposing them. If you extracted a ton of deductions, do the Must Be True/False questions first, then do the hypothetical "if" (Could Be True) questions last.

Conversely, if you could only scrape up one deduction, do the Could Be True questions first and leave the Must Be True questions for last. Skip any rule substitution questions, unless you're really good at nailing down all the questions within the time allotted. Finally, always lean toward drawing various sketches before jumping into the question sets to see all the possible worlds for the game.

Logical-Reasoning Thinking Script (Argument Questions)

Step 1: Say, "This is stupid. This author doesn't know what he's talking about." Be critical and judge harshly.

Step 2: Locate the conclusion. Is the author recommending something? Making a prediction? Comparing something? Generalizing? Making a conditional claim (an if-then statement)? Now, ask if it is strong or weak (i.e., if it has qualifiers in front of it such as *may, likely, very likely, tends to,* etc.).

Step 3: Find the evidence. This is the "why" he or she believes the conclusion above. Ex: John should do XYZ because of so-and-so reason . . . .

Step 4: Ask if the conclusion MUST, COULD, or CANNOT follow. Remember: "all" in evidence to "some" in conclusion is Must Be True, whereas "some" in evidence to "all" in conclusion is Could Be True (or Could Be False). If the conclusion cannot follow at all, then you have a logical flaw that you need to identify and match. If the conclusion doesn't necessarily follow 100% of the time, what else must the person believe or not believe for this to be true? Think about what is missing (what the assumption is) to make the two terms relevant.

Step 5: Find the assumption; it's either making the two terms relevant or introducing other possibilities, since the conclusion is on steroids. Apply the patterns learned in chapter five (e.g., assumes that two terms that appear out of nowhere are equal or not equal, generalizes from small sample size to whole, thinks there's no downside to a positive recommendation or vice versa, thinks the evidence is the only way for the conclusion to happen, says something is needed for something else, etc.).

Step 6: Also, ask how the author is arguing. Apply the patterns learned in chapter six (e.g., uses an analogy or counter-example, removes alternatives or weaknesses, says something is needed for another, etc.)

Step 7: Predict and select your answer by matching your assumption to the answer choice depending on the type of question being asked (sufficient assumption, necessary assumption, strengthen, weaken, flaw, etc.). In order to do this, first quickly eliminate wrong answer choices. For example, answer choices that introduce brand-new ideas not mentioned at all in the stimulus (e.g., the stimulus talks about smokers and answer choice mentions non-smokers), choices that compare things (uses words such as *greater than*, *less than*, or *–er* and *–est* at the end of the word), extreme answer choices (uses words such as *must, primarily, only, none, all, most*), and anything not supported at all by the stimulus.

If you have to make an assumption that is not an everyday, common-sense one, the answer choice will, most likely, be incorrect. On the harder questions, the support leading to the conclusion will be very subtle, combined with multiple viewpoints and stacked arguments (sub-conclusion, main conclusion, two pieces of evidence, two pieces of background information, etc.) and one small word can make or break the answer choice. Therefore, be extremely critical and pay close attention to details.

Reading-Comprehension Thinking Script
Reading comprehension is all about predicting what will happen paragraph by paragraph. The minute after you read the first paragraph, you need to guess what will happen next. This will help you retain the main point and structure of the passage, which will enable you to bag 50-60% of the questions just by doing this alone. The key is to identify the main point of the passage and ask yourself how each paragraph relates to the main point. You want to "push up" or link each paragraph to the author's main point.

The key is to have fun with it and be really curious. Put

yourself in the passage. Pretend you are an actor playing a role in the movie (i.e., the passage). Here is the script I used to help me conquer reading comprehension. Finally, remember that to break 150 you need to bag only 15 points (out of 27). So relax; have fun with it. Time is on your side.

Step 1: What's the point? Before my eyes lock down on even the first word, the first question that's coming into my mind is "What's the point?" Why is my time being wasted with this? Why should I care? Remind yourself what the point is in every paragraph.

Step 2: Is the author explaining or arguing? This is the second question you need to think about when your pencil touches the paper.

Step 3: What is this passage about? What's the topic?

Step 4: Say to yourself, "Oh, that's interesting. How can that be, or how can that happen?" Use this after each paragraph to stay motivated.

Step 5: Say "I agree" or "I don't agree" with the author after each paragraph and jot down what you say.

Step 6: Say "The main point of this paragraph is _____" and write it down, in just a few words.

Step 7: Say "The main purpose of this paragraph is _____" and write it down, in just a few words, after each paragraph. The purpose, as opposed to the main point (step six), should be very general, such as "to provide an example of XYZ" or "to present a hypothesis."

Step 8: Say, "The main point of entire passage is that _____" and write this down on top or the bottom of the page, after you finish reading the entire passage. This step needs to account for all paragraphs, not just the first half or the second half of the passage.

Step 9: Say, "The main purpose of the entire passage is to _____" and write this down on top or the bottom of the page, after you read the entire passage. Again, the purpose should be rather general (*to argue, to explain, to present a debate between two schools of thought, etc.*).

Step 10: Who is the author in favor of? Write this down. Usually when the author explains the passage they will present different viewpoints and side with someone.

A paragraph's function is to do one of the following: to make a claim; to propose an idea or solution; to give an example; to present an argument or a hypothesis (a single prediction or educated guess); to present a theory (a series of hypotheses); to present evidence in favor of a theory; to elaborate on a previous claim; to make relative comparisons (A versus B); to reassess previously presented info; or to refute a viewpoint (such as that of a scientist, specialist, etc.). Use one of these terms when you are going through the script above.

The best way to increase understanding and memorization is to close the test-prep book you are working from, and to get a blank piece of paper out and write down (from memory) the main point and purpose of the passage and each paragraph. In other words, if someone snatches the prep test from you the minute you finish the passage, you should be able to recall what each paragraph did and what the entire passage was about instantly. The only way this can happen is with practice.

Once you make these thinking scripts, this will become

second nature, like driving a car. When you jump in your car you don't think about putting on your seatbelt, adjusting your mirror, pressing the "push start" button, putting on your glasses, syncing your Pandora, etc. You just do it. Similarly, after putting in 480 hours of practice, you will also "just do it" naturally on the LSAT.

12

CHECK THE SCOREBOARD: BAGGING POINTS

When I ran my brokerage firm I used to say, "There is no 'E' for effort, only 'R' for results." No one cares about the effort; they only care about the results. This is how I think about the LSAT and want you to think about it. How many points did you bag? The more points you get the higher your score is—period. There are approximately 100 questions on the test. Each is worth one point and all are multiple-choice questions.

The Million-Dollar Game
Imagine now if each question were worth $10,000. If you get them all right, you just made $1,000,000. Not a bad payday for a Saturday afternoon. Okay, that's probably not going to happen—you'll be out of time before then unless you're

one of the lucky few who can finish every question within each 35-minute section. However, let's say you're not, but are happy with making $500,000 for four hours' worth of work. What would you need to do to achieve that? Get 50% of the questions right. In order to do that, you would need to know which questions to skip over and not even look at. If you have enough time to come back to them, great, but if not, within the first 45 seconds of reading it you should know (with enough practice) to completely abandon it.

In business, I used to set yearly sales goals. This year, we want to achieve $5,000,000 in gross commission income and in order to hit that, we would need to have X amount of sales associates producing Y amount in sales. Then we would work backwards (top down) and figure out our daily sales quota to make sure we were on track toward the bigger picture. However, in order to use this top-down method we needed validation that the business was viable. I'm surely not going to invest $10,000 in a Facebook pay-per-click advertising campaign with zero sales and zero proof. I would need to test it first with, let's say, $500. Once I saw proof of actual sales, I would increase the advertising budget gradually.

Treat the LSAT Like a Business

The same goes with prepping for the LSAT. In order for you to achieve your target, or top-down, score, you need to know what your calendar is going to look like monthly, weekly, daily, and hourly. It's also necessary to know your strengths and weaknesses to even plan for your calendar (i.e., the viability of *your* LSAT business). For example, if you know that parallel-reasoning questions take, on average, three minutes for you to do, with a 70/30 chance of getting each one right, why not just skip it and do two easier, less time-consuming questions with a 90/10 chance of getting it correct?

Once I realized the value in one point (e.g., $10,000), my outlook changed. When I first started testing, I used to want to beat the clock and attempt all the questions. Then I threw the clock away and did sections with unlimited time, which took hours. After about 15 full-length practice tests, I knew what questions I liked, what I disliked, what took me the most time, what took me the least time, and which questions were "hard" or "easy" in my eyes. Thus, I had a necessary foundation to be strategic about conquering the test to the best of *my* ability.

For example, the minute I have to reread the first sentence in a logical-reasoning passage or stimulus, I know the question is not for me—I'm out. This could be because the stem has very abstract language concealing the author's argument, uses double negatives, repeats single words a lot in different premises to confuse you (test-makers love doing this), or the actual answer choices are so vague that I have no idea what they are saying. Sorry, I know I'm stubborn (a personal defect), but not in today's rodeo. I'm going for the gold—the $750,000 jackpot.

How to Get Faster

In summary, know your abilities. Personally, I can hire three perfect-scoring tutors (all scoring 180 on the test) to tutor me for six months, but I know my capabilities. Will I see a large improvement in my scoring? Absolutely. Will I get a perfect score? Absolutely not. It takes me 60 seconds longer to make a deduction or work through a logical-reasoning question than it does most 160-plus high-scorers as a natural non logical thinker. That's fine. I'm slow. How do I get faster? I skip questions and focus on accuracy. If I know how to hit my target score, and that I need to answer exactly 15 correct out of 26, then I shoot for the 15 and guess on the rest. It's as simple as that.

Every question is testing you on a specific skill that law schools want you to know. They will then further refine these skills in law school and throw you out into the real world, where, one day, you may be defending someone's life. You just received a $100,000 retainer from a family that had to refinance their only asset—their home—to defend their son or daughter. Be confident in your abilities and be confident when taking the test. This comes with lots of practice and timed tests. There is a reason why your score is good for five years. The test-makers know that it takes a lot of hard work (test prep) to get through it.

The students who want that instant gratification of sitting for the test without any practice and breaking a 165 and going to their dream law school are going to get weeded out. Sure, there are outliers, and some people will be able to do that, but I'm arguing that most will not. It takes dedication, hard work, and tons of practice.

You need to be able to rip people's arguments up by pointing out logical flaws, uncovering assumptions, making inferences, weeding out the filler, strengthening or weakening the claim, and zoning into the conclusion to see if it necessarily follows from the evidence, all within less than two minutes. That's not going to happen overnight. Law schools want to see if you have what it takes to prep for six months and put in the hours. Are you willing to put in 480 hours? If so, they know you will probably do the same for each exam in law school and for passing the *bar*.

Scoring Strategy: Working Backwards

As far as strategy goes, figure out first what realistic score (based on your capabilities) you want, or how much money you want to make. If you want to make $750,000, you need to get 75% of the questions right (i.e., shoot for a 163-166 score range). There are many sites online that can convert your raw correct score to an LSAT score. This means that, if a section has 26 questions, you need 19.5 questions right (26 x .75) and 6.5 questions wrong (26 x .25). If you have 35 minutes per section, that means that you have 35 minutes / 19.5 questions = 1 minute and 79 seconds per question.

Next, practice identifying and skipping over the 6.5 "hard" questions during each practice session. This factor alone yielded me the biggest gain in my score: knowing when to let go. I was so adamant about getting every question right that I would always run out of time and only have about 60% of the questions answered, until I chose to let questions go. If you strategically figure out (after a lot of practice) which questions you will skip, you will see a tremendous improvement in your score.

In general, the easier questions vary amongst the sections. For example, in logical reasoning, the easiest are usually the first 12; then they get progressively harder. In analytical reasoning (logic games), you'll have the "could be accurate" list or "rule eliminator" questions that are usually first in each game. In reading comprehension, you will have the big-picture questions and detail questions, such as, "Which of the following most accurately states the main point of the passage?" or "According to the passage . . . ?"

These are all questions you want to attack first, and skip those that you find challenging. Challenging can mean too time-consuming or too confusing to understand. Whatever you realize is killing your score during your practice sessions is what you want to let go; "cut your losses short," as they say in the business world. Stick to the winners and bag points.

Finally, remember that your end score is like money—it's a scorecard. It's a measure of your hard work and the effort you put in up front. If you cold-call and knock on enough doors, you will see an increase in sales. Similarly, if you do hours of practice and review, you will see a higher score. Both, however, depend on the fundamentals: market viability and the core LSAT strategies mastered in this book and your future test-prep courses. If you strategically approach the test, selecting which questions to do and not do, then you will crush it on test day. Bag as many points as you can and check the scoreboard a couple of weeks later. How much money did you make? Drop me a tweet (@shahofmiami) and let me know.

13

HOW TO REVIEW YOUR PRACTICE TESTS THE RIGHT WAY

So, you do your first practice test on Saturday morning. After spending four hours or so, you go take a break and then anxiously come back to turn to the back of the book and see how many questions you bubbled in correctly. You are now thinking, "Yes, I knew I was I was right" or "Wow, I can't believe I chose that answer." Then, the next Saturday, you repeat the same drill and end up with the same results. What does this iterative process prove? That you seek instant gratification. The most important process after spending so many hours training for the LSAT is your review process. Here's one of the most effective ways to see strong gains from one practice test to the next.

First, do only one full-length (five sections) practice test a week. If you don't have an "experimental section," just throw one in from another Prep Test; meanwhile, during the week, focus on repetition of question types and individual sections. If you do practice tests back to back, the only thing you are working on is stamina. Although it's good, the tradeoff for burning through fresh LSAT material is not worth it; there are only 77 official LSAT Prep Tests for you to work on (to date).

Next, during the actual practice test, if you are not 100-percent certain why a certain answer is correct, then circle the question. For example, if you get down to two answer choices, then circle it. If you can only eliminate three out of five answer choices, then circle the question also. There is only one answer choice that is correct and four incorrect ones. Thus, there is something wrong with each answer choice that makes it wrong. If you cannot find it, then circle the question.

Now it's time to review your answer choices; reprint the entire test and do the following in order with unlimited time: first the questions you skipped entirely, then the questions you circled. Finally, check both answers with a thorough explanation answer key from whichever test-prep company you are studying with. If you got the untimed question correct it could be that you simply misread under timed conditions and that threw you off or you were anxious and let the stress get to you. If your first answer choice was correct and under untimed review you got it wrong, then that tells you something valuable: you didn't really understand the question.

So, analyze exactly what trap you fell for to avoid that again. Since the LSAT is a standardized test, you will see patterns of wrong answers (as well as right answers) over and over again. See Appendix I. These are great to skip, or go back and practice drills of that question type.

This method of reviewing your answers the correct way is arduous and laborious. Some of my reviews would take over two hours for just one section. However, it works. If you really want to see results and want to break out of your LSAT plateau that everyone eventually reaches, then review thoroughly with unlimited time. Remember: nothing worth it comes easy. Go hard!

14

THE 15-POINT TRIAGE RULE

You have 30 seconds to decide: save yourself or save a life of a two-year-old? There exists no other possibility or option. What do you do? Okay, so this type of decision-making will definitely not be needed on test day, although it can feel as intense. The act of knowing which questions not to do plays a necessary role in breaking 150 on the LSAT. The test-makers' goal is to see if you can crack under pressure. How do they do this? They sprinkle very time-consuming questions throughout the test.

When I took the real test in October of 2015, I remember walking out of there as if the test-makers had abused me. They threw in a very hard inference question early on in the logical-reasoning section and I was stunned. Also, the guy making a hole in his desk with his eraser didn't help. The problem with me is that I'm a perfectionist, so it's hard for me to let go at times. This is especially true for the second question of the entire test. As a result, I froze and everything I had learned seemed to go out the window on section one. Luckily, on sections two, three, and four I gained my composure and held it together. So, to avoid repeating my experience, you must realize when not to do a question and move on.

The same goes for reading comprehension. Imagine starting a reading-comp section and the test-makers give you a hard philosophy or science passage and then by the time you spend five minutes on it, you see the questions set and determine that there are zero big-picture, main-point questions and nothing but parallel and analogy questions. You just burned five to six precious minutes that you could have saved for the end by taking on easier passages and questions up front.

How to Bag 15 Points in Reading Comprehension
The test-makers' job is to intentionally throw "speed bumps" in your test to get you off your rhythm. So, the question is: will you let the test control you or will you control the test? In order to do the latter, you need to be strategic about exactly which passage you are going to do and which question you are going to do first. Starting with reading comprehension, since we are on the subject, the first thing you should do is take one minute (out of 35) and write "1, 2, 3, 4" to determine in which order you will do the passages. Many times, the order of doing passages from easiest to hardest falls into "1, 2, 4, 3" or "1, 2, 3, 4," but it's still subjective.

You do this by reading the first sentence of each passage. Do you completely understand it, or understand most of it, some of it, or none of it? If it's not all or most, mark this off for later. Next, look at the paragraphs. Is there a clear structure? For example, is the first sentence of each paragraph the main point followed by supporting evidence (1, 2, 3, 4)? Are there a lot of opinionated keywords (*I suggest, clearly, essential, should*, etc.)? How about contrast keywords (*but, yet, however*)? Finally, look at the questions and check off the three to four you will do; take the time to physically draw a check mark next to these questions.

FOCUS ON BIG-PICTURE, DETAIL, AND INFERENCE QUESTIONS

For example, what I do is check off any "big-picture" questions, or anything that asks me for the main point, for the author's attitude, or to describe the structure. Next, I check off any "detail questions" that ask me to go back to the passage, and "inference questions" where I can point my finger to the line where it's asking me to find a Must Be True answer. The detail questions start with "according to the passage," while the inference questions usually start off with "based on the passage." Finally, I don't check off (i.e., I leave unmarked) any parallel-reasoning, or strengthen/weaken questions, as those are generally harder and more time-consuming. Also, if there are no line references in the question, I skip those as well.

So, to sum up, as the clock starts, I turn to passage one,

THE 15-POINT TRIAGE RULE

take a quick glance after reading the first sentence of the passage, and check off three or four questions that I will do, and then repeat this for passages two, three, and four. Then I'll write at the top of my booklet the order "1, 2, 4, 3" and start. Did I burn a few minutes? Sure, but guess what? I gained confidence. I am now in control of the test. This is how you take charge of the reading-comp section.

Next, to break 150 on the LSAT, your goal is to get 15 right per section. For reading comprehension, you should actually attempt 16-18 questions and leave around eight to ten (out of 27 total) for pure, blind guessing. So the way to do this is by doing at least three out of four passages, but doing only five out of six or seven questions. Take three minutes to read each passage, underline/box main points etc., and then approximately six minutes for the questions. Your goal is to only do five questions per passage (as opposed to six or seven).

If the passage "feels" hard, just do four questions and move on to the next one. Your job is only to attempt at least 16 total. The biggest trap the LSAT makers present you with is throwing in time-draining questions. Also, they will put hard questions in every passage; they know the game. So focus on bagging your five questions and move on as soon as you see nine minutes spent on the clock per section.

After completing three passages, you will have around five or six minutes left to attempt to do at least two or three questions on the last passage and guess. The questions you want to do again are big-picture (*main point, organization, author attitude,* etc.), detail (*according to the passage*) and inference (*suggests, inferred,* etc.) questions, where you can basically point your finger to a line in the passage and figure out which answer choice must be true.

Blind-Guessing Strategy

For the remaining eight to ten questions that you don't have time to look at, you simply pick one letter and bubble in the same letter all the way down the answer sheet (e.g., DDDDD). However, be strategic about this. I look at my answer sheet and see which letter is used less and go with that one. I noticed, after doing all 77 Prep Tests, that the LSAT will not use a letter more than seven times in a row for a section. So, if you notice a high frequency of the letter "D," then don't use that to guess. Of course, this assumes that you answered the questions correctly. Your guessing goal is to get one or two extra guess points. Anything over 15 can make up for incorrect answer choices, or just be a bonus.

Reading-Comp Strategy (15 points)

- Attempt 16-18 questions (out of 27).
- Do three passages, five questions per passage.
- For the last passage, do two or three questions and then "blind-guess" strategically.
- Take three minutes to read and six minutes for questions on all passages and do the big picture, detail, and inference questions in that order.
- For blind guessing, look at your answer sheet and see which letter you used less frequently. If you bubbled in letter "D" only three times, while you bubbled in

the other letters more frequently (e.g., four to seven times), use letter "D" to bubble in for the last passage (e.g., DDDDDD). Your goal is to get one or two freebies on this passage.

How to Bag 15 Points in Logic Games

Next, let's talk about logic games. The great thing about games is that you get better with practice. Arguably, this is probably the easiest section to improve, as there is one concrete answer. Many people claim massive amounts of improvements on this section with time, since there are only so many ways test-makers can throw games and rules at you. Because the rules are finite, repetition is the answer for speed as you internally memorize how to make deductions faster with each time you do a game. If you set the board and rules up right, only one exact answer fits—just like a math equation. That is why, unlike reading comprehension, you will have a much higher accuracy and for this section your goal is to attempt to bag 15/23 questions.

FOCUS ON THE SINGLE-ACTION GAMES

In this section, you will usually see two easier games and two harder games. Generally the one-action games with only one entity are the easiest (e.g., ordering, grouping just one variable set). Again, the goal is to get 15 points (out of approximately 23). So, you want to do these two easier games first. Usually there are five or six questions per game and you will want to bag five points each for these two easier games, for a total of 10 points. These easier games should not take you longer than eight or nine minutes. When I first started doing the "easy" games I was doing them in 25 minutes each. Over time, and with practice, I got my time down to 15, then 10, and then eight minutes. It's all about repetition, as your mind brings from memory what you have to do for a specific type of game (e.g., in loose ordering, figuring out which entity can be first or last).

So, as with reading comprehension, your first task is to determine the order in which you will attempt the games. What I do is glance at each game and see which games require just one action (e.g., only ordering or only grouping). That's what I'm doing first. Next, I determine which games require two actions or have complicated rules—those I am doing last. This gives me a sense of each game, of what I'm being asked to do (order, group, etc.), and of what's involved (how many entities there are). Then I write down which I want to do first at the top of my booklet (e.g., 1, 2, 4, 3) and get started. As far as difficulty goes, remember that one entity and one action will be easier than juggling two different entities and two different actions.

In terms of individual questions, knock out all the "rule eliminator questions," if provided, first, as they are the low-hanging fruit and an opportunity to bag an easy four points for the section. That's the question that is usually the first one in the set and starts with "Which one of the following could be an accurate list of . . . ?" Also, instead of checking off which questions I will do (as in reading comp), I actually "X" off which questions I'm not going to do because there are a lot of Must Be True and Could Be True questions, the difficulty of which depends on the game. For example, "rule substitution" and "completely determined questions" I'm not even looking at; I'm putting a big fat "X" on the entire question. If I have time, I'll do that last.

Once you complete both games, you will have about eight or nine minutes for the next two "hard games." You want to pick the less difficult one and do this one first. Do the "acceptability" question and do a "Could Be True" question, as you don't have to do multiple sub-games or sketches, as is the case with a "Must Be True" question. Your goal is get as many points as you can. I managed to bag two or three, then I just forced myself to move on to the last game. Every game will give you one or two easy questions, so don't be stubborn and stay stuck. Finally, with blind guessing, use the same strategy of picking an answer choice that is used least on your answer sheet.

Logic-Games Strategy (15 points)

- Attempt 15 questions (out of 23).
- Do all four games (eight or nine minutes per game).
- Do five questions on the first two "easier" games (total of 10/13).
- Do only two or three questions on the next two "harder" games (5-6/13), leaving each game in eight or nine minutes, no matter what.
- Pick the one letter used least on the answer sheet and use it to bubble in remaining 8 questions (e.g., EEEEEE).

How to Bag 15 Points in Logical Reasoning

Finally comes logical reasoning. First, you can't really go through each question beforehand and check or "X," as there are about 25-26 questions and it will burn too much time (in excess of five minutes). So, instead you want to do the questions in order from page one. Now, your goal, again, is to attempt 18 questions but bag only 15 (out of 25/26). But remember: the test-makers will throw speed bumps in throughout the test. Generally, logical reasoning gets progressively harder from question one to question 26.

THE CHUNKING STRATEGY

So, start at question one and circle your task. If the question stem says "resolve," I'm circling that. If it says "role," I'm circling that. If it says "logically completes," I'm circling that inference question. Since there are two pages of questions, look to your right and see if there are any matching question types. For example, if the question stem says "role" in question one, is there another "role" question to your right (without you flipping the page), let's say in question seven? If so, do them both in pairs. This way, you're already thinking about "role" strategy and you don't have to mentally shift from "role" to "inference" to "strengthen" and back to "role" again.

This "chunking" strategy gives you a big advantage over your competition. It gives you a "preview" of the questions as opposed to just doing them as the test-makers set them up for you to do them. Do you like the feeling of going into a batting cage, for example, and not knowing which ball is going to be flying out of the machine (curveball, fastball, slider, etc.)? I sure don't. Take control of the test.

THE MAIN-POINT MANTRA

Next, if you don't understand the question within 45 seconds after reading it, move on. There are too many easy points waiting for you later (e.g., "main point" questions) to get stuck on one or two questions and burn five or six minutes on it with a great chance of getting it wrong anyways. Always have this mantra in the back of your mind: *There is an easier question waiting for me.*

Finally, never spend more than two minutes per question: one minute to understand the argument and one minute to eliminate the wrong answers and pick the right answer. For example, 15 questions x two minutes gives you approximately 30 minutes, with five minutes remaining to do two or three more questions and go back and guess on the rest.

This is exactly what I did when I took the test in December of 2015. As I went from question one through question 26, I circled matching question types and did them in chunks on pages one and two. When I turned the page, I did the same. So, if I saw a flaw question, I did that, then quickly searched for the next flaw question and on to the next, etc. I repeated this pattern across all question types.

For me, the "hard" questions were those with two or three arguments stacked on top of each other (e.g., scientists' arguments, or authors or ethicists, or critics and authors). Also, I noticed that the heavier the use of modifiers, pronouns, and abstract language, the harder the question is going to be. The easy questions almost hit you in the face with the answer. Conversely, the hard questions are hard in the argument and the answer choices (or both). So once I recognized that this was a hard question, I moved on. I did not blind-guess on the spot. I skipped it entirely. For a good indication of time-consuming questions check out Appendix B at the back of this book so you get a sense of which ones to skip, unless you absolutely dominate them and want to knock it out early.

The point is that you must get through every question with speed and accuracy. You deserve to at least see every question and make a decision as to whether to do it or not. Thus, skip by choice, not by force. Keep your tempo going. Once you find the right answer, do not double-guess yourself. Pick it, and move.

Finally, for guessing, figure out which letter you bubbled in the least and fill up the page with that, in the hopes of bagging an additional one or two points. It's important to not guess on the spot and finish your set of 18 questions and take a look at your answer sheet to see which letter is used least. This will give you an advantage over your competitors who simply blind-guess on the spot if they don't know the answer. Be strategic.

What really slows you down in logical reasoning is not understanding the argument because of the extra layer of fluff the test-makers put on it. Some people claim that the hard questions are bunched up between questions 14 and 21, and the last couple of questions are the easiest. However, other people feel differently. I personally noticed that the middle of the logical-reasoning section gets extremely hard and for whatever reason, the test-makers tend to use "B" as a popular answer choice for harder questions. This is based on my findings from doing all of the practice tests and, of course, is not representative of everyone's experience. Regardless, just go with an answer choice that's bubbled in the least and you will be fine.

If you simply go in order, one to 26, and quickly skip over what you don't understand, or skip over questions with terms such as *ethicist, philosopher,* etc., then you will dominate this game. Likewise, if you do the question in chunks and practice it to touch at least 18 logical-reasoning sections, you will master it on test day. Create a habit so on test day everything is instinct. At the end of the day, this is what the LSAT is all about; how many more points can you get than your competition? Always control the test and don't let it control you.

Logical-Reasoning Strategy (15 points)

- Touch 18 questions (out of 25/26), with no more than two minutes per question.
- Do questions in order: 1-26.
- Do questions in "chunks" on the same page (e.g., Q1 Flaw and Q7 Flaw)

- Skip the question completely within 45 seconds if you don't understand it or recognize that it will be a hard question.
- Pick the one letter least used on the answer sheet and use to bubble in remaining 10 or 11 questions (e.g., DDDDDD).

15

FINAL WORDS

Congrats on making it to the finale. I hope you are excited to tackle your LSAT prep course or actual test, whenever that shall be. In the end, prepping for the LSAT is a long and arduous battle. It's not for the instant-gratification seekers or the non-thick-skinned. It will knock you on your butt, make you cry, make you doubt yourself, and tailspin you into a mild depression. At times you will get simple questions wrong and will feel like you want to do 20 more questions out of frustration, just like a gambler losing money on a big hand to wants to play again to lose even more money. Don't worry—these symptoms are normal, and the only cure is time and practice (for the LSAT, of course).

The LSAT's purpose is to train you to think a certain way and then test you to think that way within a short period of time. You must keep your cool and focus on the strategies; never let the LSAT, or "house" at a casino, win. The good thing is that this game can be beaten. How long it will take you is the question, and will you decide to give up or stick with it until your mind starts eating, sleeping, and breathing LSAT? Just like any skilled-based sport, the LSAT is mastered by first learning the proper fundamentals and then practicing religiously until every strategy becomes instinct to you.

I remember specifically during the December 2015 LSAT that I had a very tricky main-point question. It was question number 10 and the LSAT makers placed the correct answer as "B" right underneath a very attractive trap answer choice, "A." Because of my experience with the test and doing countless main-point questions I had a gut instinct to not pick A through experience (i.e., time). I was right. My buddy at the time, unfortunately, chose A.

I remember talking about it with him after the test and he was just as adamant that the answer was A as I was that it was B. He only had three months of prep, as opposed to my six. This shows you that doing countless practice tests can give you that advantage just like when the lights are on, it's game four of the championship finals with twenty-four seconds left on the clock, and all eyes are on you as you are about to shoot the game-winning jump shot.

If you ask yourself, "Does the conclusion necessarily follow from the evidence?" every time you read an argument, you will become an LSAT champ. That should trigger a series of questions about whether the evidence is relevant or not, what the missing link (assumption) is that's needed to help out the

Olympic long jumper, or if the evidence and conclusion are relevant but extreme, to find an alternative possibility such as "you must do X." Then you can identify the assumption, strengthen, weaken, or match the flaw.

Similarly, by sticking close to the fact set and combining duplicate terms and forming contrapositives, you can deduce what Must Be True and what Must Be False in logic games. Finally, by reading for main point and structure and then going back to the passage as a researcher when asked, you can dominate the reading-comprehension section.

By asking and doing these series of questions day in and day out, truly internalizing the material and applying it until your LSAT test day, you will rewire your brain to think the way the test-makers want you to. In the end, your hard work and dedication should yield you at least a 10 to 15-point gain, depending on your starting point, your dedication, and your hard work. Hopefully this is sufficient to break 150 on your big day.

I hope you found tremendous value in this book. I spend countless hours writing, rewriting, and condensing the material down to what really mattered conceptually to aid me in taking a step back and seeing the LSAT from more than just doing practice problems over and over again. I know you're going to see thousands of LSAT problems in the next three to six months (or more), so on the days when you are "burned out" reread this manuscript; it will serve as a savory refresher.

In the end, I can look back to when I first started and say that I went from having a fearful hatred view of the LSAT to being a loving LSAT connoisseur (see Appendix H). I went from being massively overwhelmed to slowly grasping the fundamental concepts (such as formal logic), to realizing that, in the end, LSAT mastery can be summed up in two broad-stroke tactics: attack the assumption and find the Must Be True deductions.

When I was first exposed to the test my attitude was "I just want to get into any law school." With gaining confidence and seeing results I shifted to "Okay, maybe I can score somewhat decent and get some scholarship money." Finally, towards the end of my practice, my attitude did a complete 180. I was thinking, "Okay, how can I get a perfect score—a 180—on this test"?

However, the most important benefit that I gained by investing my energy and 480-plus hours into this test was the ability to think logically, to think like a lawyer. I stopped agreeing and disagreeing with people and learned how to objectively evaluate arguments. It made me smarter and sharper, and enabled me to have another skill set under my belt. If you were anything like me starting out, not even knowing what an assumption was 180 days ago, then I'm confident that it will do the same for you, if it hasn't already.

The best part of your long journey will be to get that acceptance letter to not one but several schools of your choice (see Appendix J). Most importantly, it will be to get a surprise merit-scholarship offer and become part of the "haves" instead of the "have-nots" of the law-school business model. It's exciting and so rewarding. Stay focused, put in the hard work, and be confident on test day so you can crush the LSAT. See you in law school!

APPENDIX A: The Secret Language of Lawyers

Below are some examples of the secret language of lawyers, written for lawyers and by lawyers only. It enables them to create a way to think and speak so only they can be understood, thereby creating a needed service in the marketplace. Make sure you master these sufficient and necessary conditions cold before sitting for the actual LSAT. After all, you will be part of the club, so you might as well get a head start now. I underlined the necessary portions of the conditions below:

- If P, <u>then Q</u>
- <u>Q</u> if P
- P <u>only if Q</u>
- <u>Only P</u> are Q
- <u>P if, but only if Q</u> (both are sufficient and necessary for each other—"BFFs")

- <u>P if, and only if Q</u> (both are sufficient and necessary for each other—"BFFs")
- The only P is <u>Q</u>
- Not P <u>unless Q</u>
- P <u>unless Q</u>
- <u>Unless Q</u>, no P
- <u>Unless Q</u>, P
- No P <u>without Q</u>
- No P <u>until Q</u>
- Not P or Not Q <u>unless Z</u>
- If P <u>then Q or Z, but not both</u>

APPENDIX B: Time-Draining Questions on the LSAT

Below are the questions that usually take longer than one minute and 30 seconds for me. This doesn't necessarily make them difficult. If you cannot finish no matter what and after however many months of practice, then skip these and come back to them if you have time. Be smart about it.

You will skip questions eventually, whether you like it or not. For example, if you only do questions 1-18 then you inadvertently skipped 19-25. What if the last six were the easiest? What if they were easier than questions 12-18, of which you got 50% wrong. You see what I mean? Be strategic about what you're going to skip. Always ask, "Is this question worth my time? Is it a good return on my investment of time?" Remember that each question is worth one point. It doesn't make sense to spend three minutes on a question to gain one point when you can skip and spend one minute and 30 seconds on two questions and bag two points.

One more critical thing: know your capabilities. Only by

knowing exactly how long it takes for you to do each type of question will you be cognizant of what you should and should not skip. This includes factoring in an accuracy level (e.g., X right out of 10). If you're getting eight out of 10 right all the time on an inference problem, for example, then do it. If you are getting only five out of 10 right on a parallel-flaw problem, then you may lean towards skipping it, as you're batting at 50%. It's not like on test day you will magically get eight out of 10 right; not likely. Here is an example of my time and accuracy on each question type below. Once I took a step back and realized this I had my final "a-ha" moment, a true mastery of the LSAT:

APPENDIX B: TIME-DRAINING QUESTIONS ON THE LSAT

LOGICAL-REASONING Time-Drainers (in BOLD)

ARGUMENTS
- **Assumption: Sufficient**
- Assumption: Necessary
- Strengthen/Weaken
- Evaluate
- Flaw
- Main Point
- Strategy Role Questions
- Strategy Technique Questions
- **Parallel Reasoning**
- **Parallel Flaw**
- **Point at Issue**
- **Principle**

NON-ARGUMENTS (FACT SET)
- **Inference (MBT, MBF)**
- Resolve Discrepancy

READING-COMP Time-Drainers (in BOLD)

- Big Picture
- Detail with Keywords
- Inference with Keywords
- **Open ended: No Keywords in answer choice for you to research**
- Analogy
- **Strengthen/Weaken**
- **Logic Reasoning Type**

ANALYTICAL-REASONING/ LOGIC-GAMES Time-Drainers (In BOLD)

ONE ENTITY SET
- Ordering (Strict, Loose)
- Matching
- Grouping I (Select, Distribute)

TWO-ENTITY SET
- **Grouping II (Select, Distribute)**
- **Hybrid (two actions)**

APPENDIX C: Know Your Capabilities—Timing with Accuracy

This will be different for everyone. In order for you to know your capabilities, do at least 10 questions in a row of each type per day. This includes all levels of difficulty. Since you really don't know which one is difficult or not to include, do both easy and hard ones. In other words, don't exclude easy or hard questions if you are aware of them.

Generally, harder questions have multiple arguments in the stimulus (e.g., critic's and author's) in logical reasoning or really abstract answer choices that all sound the same. In reading comp, you'll find a lack of keywords or opinions, making it difficult to follow along with the structure. In logic games, you will find multiple actions and entities that make it hard to nail down the sketch. Also, harder games have very open-ended rules (i.e., not pinning down variables), and have questions that make you draw at least two sub-games or options out, thus quenching your time.

So to begin, start a timer and pause it after you finish your

APPENDIX C: KNOW YOUR CAPABILITIES—TIMING WITH ACCURACY

repetition ("reps") of ten or more. Don't look at the answers until after you complete your reps; also pause the timer after each question is completed to jot down the time. After ten questions, for example, take the average of your times. So if you did 10 logical-reasoning inference questions and it took you 2:15, 2:50: 3:30, 4:05, etc., take the average to assess your time. Repeat this exercise as often as you can to see, a couple of weeks from now, if you're improving or not. You can also go online to find a free stopwatch to (Google "online stop watch") that makes sounds so you can set up intervals while you practice (e.g., at three minutes after a passage is done or one minute and 30 seconds after a logical reasoning problem is done). You need to get a sense of what finishing a section feels like before you sit for the real test. Otherwise, you may be missing very easy questions at the end, which you could have bagged quickly if you would have gotten to them.

The minute I forced myself to go through each question in the allocated time (e.g., one minute and 30 seconds) I got a gut intuition after doing a section daily so that on the real tests it was automatic for me. If I didn't figure it out within 45 seconds of reading it, I just circled the answer and moved on. If I was one minute and 25 seconds in and down to two answer choices, I guessed and moved on. This was when I saw a real breakthrough in my score. Timing is just as important than accuracy (if not more so). It's a skill that must be practiced.

APPENDIX D: Common Evidence and Conclusion Patterns

EVIDENCE	CONCLUSION	OLYMPIC JUMP
X can happen.	X will happen.	Can doesn't equal will.
A happened; B happened.	A causes B.	Saying there is no other possibility other than A. What about C? What if B actually makes A happen? What if D and A make B happen?
X, then Y.	Got home, saw Y, so X.	Something that was needed or dependent is now a powerhouse trigger (i.e. sufficient)
Z is cheap.	We should buy Z.	Overlooks any downside risk that may outweigh being cheap (e.g., you can die by using it).

APPENDIX D: COMMON EVIDENCE AND CONCLUSION PATTERNS

EVIDENCE	CONCLUSION	OLYMPIC JUMP
W corp. has a risky division.	Don't loan to them.	Overlooks any upside risks, like their overall portfolio, from having zero risk OR we can secure all their business with this deal, which outweighs the risk.
A is serious.	So, I like A.	Assumes serious = like (equal)
A is not serious.	So, I like A.	Assumes not serious = like (not equal)
A is not serious.	So, I don't like A.	Assumes liking A is needed to be serious (needed).

EVIDENCE	CONCLUSION	OLYMPIC JUMP
Three widgets are bad.	All widgets are bad.	Three represents all (part to whole fallacy).
A believes X to happen.	So, X will happen.	Belief doesn't equal fact (flaw).
50% increase/decrease in sales	$500 dollars more/less made	% up/down doesn't mean absolute number up/down (flaw)
Person is a bad speaker	Not voting for him	**Ad hominem** attack-attacks the person not the argument (flaw)

EVIDENCE	CONCLUSION	OLYMPIC JUMP
Can't prove there is no X.	So, X.	Failure to disprove = Proof (flaw)
Dr. Psychologist said so.	So you have cancer (Z).	Wrong authority (not MD) (flaw)
X because Y.	No, X because Z.	Avoids argument/question—ignores evidence (flaw)
W is up, and Y is down.	W made Y go down.	Correlation doesn't equal causation (flaw).
X caused Y.	Z didn't cause Y, so no Y.	Z could also cause Y. X alone isn't the only way (flaw). Inaccurately assumes X is necessary.
X caused Y (which is bad).	So, A or B as solution.	Could be other ways to fix issue (flaw).
X is Y.	So, X ought to/should be done.	"Is" is describing something whereas "ought to/should" is prescribing something; not taking downside risk into consideration.
X or Y.	So not X, therefore Y.	It should be X and not X or Y and not Y for a true binary cut (false-dichotomy flaw).
One group (X) dislikes Y.	So, everyone dislikes Y.	Small sample to general (flaw).

APPENDIX D: COMMON EVIDENCE AND CONCLUSION PATTERNS

EVIDENCE	CONCLUSION	OLYMPIC JUMP
Group 1 has X trait and Group 2 doesn't have it.	So, not X.	Assumes X only characteristic for all group; overlooks other possibilities (flaw).
You have a legal right.	You have no rights at all.	Equivocation. Uses rights in two different ways (flaw).
PPL agree we should decrease X.	So, we should decrease X.	No evidence to back up claim; assumes X is high (flaw).
PPL believe X is true.	X is false because a scientist manipulated the data.	One sample represents all; overgeneralization (flaw).
X and Y agree to do Z.	X accepts, so Z.	Assumes Y also agrees.

APPENDIX E: Logic-Games Homework—Practice Drills by Question Type

If you want to ace the logic-games section, before taking your actual LSAT, complete every single logic game type below. Find a PrepTest and look for the appropriate game (strict sequence, loose sequence, selection, matching, grouping). Next, do each type of game at least five times in a row.

The key is to have your brain repeat making inferences until it's second nature and that only comes with repetition. The minute you start doing the game over and over again, you are going to see great strides in not only your accuracy but, most importantly, timing. If you are not finishing each game in under nine minutes, or not getting every question correct within the time limit, then don't leave this type of game.

APPENDIX E: LOGIC-GAMES HOMEWORK—PRACTICE DRILLS BY QUESTION TYPE

Formal Logic Statement

~ F < 8:30 **or** ~ 100% correct ➜ ~ Leave Game Type

If you Leave Game Type ➜ F < 8:30 **and**
got 100% correct (contrapositive)

From the homework assignment below, the ones in bold are my personal favorite games:

Logic Games Strict Sequencing
Prep Test Homework:
3, 4, 5, 6, 7, 8, 11, 12, 13, 15, 16, 17, 18, 19, 20, 21, 23, **24**, 25, **26**, **27**, **28**, **29**, 30, 31, 32, 34, 35, 37, 39, 40, 41, 42, **43**, 44, 45, 46, 47, **49**, 50, 54, 55, 56, **57**, 58, **59**, 60, 61, 62, 63, **64**, 65, 67, **68**, 69, 72, FEB 97, June 2007, Super Test A

Notes with Strict Sequencing:
- <u>Entities:</u> one set
- <u>Action:</u> Order entities into slots.
- <u>Hints to Know Game Type</u>: *order, sequence, rank, successively, consecutively, immediately before or immediately after, one in each space*
- <u>Think About</u>: connecting the rules together and form building blocks like Legos from matching entities. For example: Take "M," mentioned in rules 1 and 3, then combine them and form a block. Next, fit these block chunks into your sketch. If you have two sets of blocks that need to fit into a sketch that means the game will be restrictive.

- Usually those two sets of blocks (AG_W and DH_S) will not be able to be placed in the middle of the sketch as that will force the other block to not fit in the diagram. Next, if a rule says "M" can go in 3 or 5, then immediately draw out two sketches and place all the other entities around it. Figure out what CANNOT go where and what MUST go where. Finally, think about the entities that have no rules talking about them (i.e., are floaters). These can go anywhere and are great for CBT questions; on MBT questions floaters can never be the correct choice as there are no rules that mandate that they do something or don't do something.
- <u>Tips:</u> Create two or three possibilities (sketches) from the beginning if possible. However, if many possibilities exist (i.e., entities are not fixed) just move to the questions fast. Don't spin your wheels trying to squeeze out inferences. Next, with multiple sketches you are creating "Could Be True" or "possible" scenarios. If you see an entity (e.g., X), always in a certain position in all of your possible scenarios (3 sketches), then you know that "MBT" all the time.

    If you have a slot with a lot of entities that cannot go there (i.e., negatives), focus on that first. Remember: with MBT answers, the wrong answers are MBF and CBF. Make sure to test quickly the remaining answer choices to validate your answer; otherwise, if you move too quickly, you might have just picked a CBT answer choice. Finally, to save time with "if" CBT questions (e.g., if N is in 3rd then . . .) put N in third and quickly look to the rules to see which rules trigger when that happens. If you have

APPENDIX E: LOGIC-GAMES HOMEWORK—PRACTICE DRILLS BY QUESTION TYPE

two or three possibilities, stack the two or three scenarios on top of each other instead of copying out the entire sketch. So RSNT and another RTNS on top of it to figure out what Could Be True to save time.

Finally, for "fully determined questions," go down the answer choices and see which sketch it's referring to. For example, if the answer choice says, "S is shown second," find the game sketch where that applies and see if all the other entities are fixed in place. If any of them can float around, then it's not fully determined. Also, if "S" is shown in second in more than one sketch, it's not fully determined.

- <u>Sketch:</u> Use dash lines _ _ _ _

Question Strategy:
1. Do rule elimination first.
2. Do "if/CBT questions" second.
3. Do if MBT/MBF third. (Do sub-game sketches to see all options.)
4. Do MBT/MBF open-ended fourth. (Look at other sub-game sketches to eliminate answers.) Note: here you will have to test each answer choice. Don't start with any floaters (i.e., no rules mention the floater entity so it can't be a "Must Be" by default).
5. Skip rule-substitution questions, if running out of time.
6. If you see "complete determined question," test the entity not mentioned in the rules (i.e., floater) first. Also test the most restricted rule first. For example, if there is a chain (e.g. F—H—I), test I (someone at end of chain)

in an earlier position to fix all the other slots in an ordering game.
7. If you see "complete and accurate list" it's like a rule-elimination question. Test each rule and eliminate.

Logic Games Double Sequencing Prep Test Homework (same strategies as above):
24, 32, 38, 69, 72, 74, 75

Logic Games Loose Sequencing Prep Test Homework:
1, 2, 4, 6, 7, 10, 14, 33, 38, **42**, **43**, 48, **51**, **52**, 53, **55**, 60, 61, 65, 71, 73, 74, 75, B, C

Notes with Loose Sequencing:
- Entities: one set
- Action: Order entities into slots loosely.
- Hints to Know Game Type: *order, sequence, rank, X before or after Y, above or below one another, highest and lowest.* If the adjective ends with an "-er" it's loose (e.g., higher, lower).
- Think About: Relative positions. Who can go first? Who can go last? When you put one entity in, count the number of people who can go before and after that person. So, when you're asked about who can go into an early position you eliminate anyone that is at the end of the chain; if asked who can go at the end, you eliminate anyone who is at the beginning of the chain. Also, create possible options (sketches) early to determine what Must Be True and Could Be True. I like to circle the entities

APPENDIX E: LOGIC-GAMES HOMEWORK—PRACTICE DRILLS BY QUESTION TYPE

that can possibly go first, and box the entities that can go last. Anything not circled or boxed cannot lead or follow the chain. (They are stuck in the middle.)
- <u>Tips:</u> Create two possibilities (sketches) from the beginning if possible. These are Could Be True scenarios. If there are no fixed rules, such as "N can go in either 3 or 4," and the game is a pure relative-sequencing game, link up the rules immediately to save time instead of jotting them all down and then going back and linking them up. Again, pay attention to any entities that are not mentioned in the rules, as these are "floaters" and can go anywhere. Thus, any MBT or MBF question mentioning a floater is going to be wrong, as there is no mandate on it.

    Conversely, any CBT/CBF question is going to test your ability to understand the floater, so plug that into the sketch first and see what happens. Finally for "fully determined questions," look to try the entity in the answer choice that is connected with a lot of rules and thus triggers a lot of actions in the game.
- <u>Sketch:</u> Use spider web/tree A—B—D---E---G

Question Strategy:
1. Do rule elimination first.
2. Do "if/CBT questions" second.
3. Do if MBT/MBF third. (Do sub-game boards to see all options.)
4. Do MBT/MBF open-ended fourth. (Look at other sub-game boards to eliminate answers.) Note: here you will have to test each answer choice. Don't start with any

floaters (i.e., no rules mention the floater entity so it can't be a "must be" by default).

5. Skip rule substitution questions, if running out of time.
6. If you see "complete determined question," test the entity not mentioned in the rules (i.e., floater) first. Also, test the most restricted rule first.
7. If you see "complete and accurate list" it's like a rule-elimination question. Test each rule and eliminate.

Logic Games Grouping I (Selection)
Prep Test Homework:
5, 8, 9, 11, 20, 23, 24, **25**, 26, 31, 32, 33, **34**, 35, 36, 39, 40, 41, 42, **45**, 47, 48, **49**, 50, 54, **58**, 59, **64, 65,** 70, A, B

Notes with Selection:
- Entities: one set
- Action: Select entities (in or out).
- Hints to Know Game Type: *select, pick, choose, determine*, or if you see the rules with formal logic in them
- Think About: Who is on the team? Who is out? Does the entire team need to be full? Can a team be empty? Who's NOT selected? Think about numbers (minimums and maximums allowed in groups). A very common rule will have an *or* in it, indicating that either one or the other is in (maybe both). For example: If X or Y is in group A that means: If Not X then Y is in; if not Y, then X is in. This means that group A cannot be empty; at least one must be in. Also, if the question asks "Which pair of entities cannot both be out?" look to your "or pair," as one of these

APPENDIX E: LOGIC-GAMES HOMEWORK—PRACTICE DRILLS BY QUESTION TYPE

variables must always be in. Notice how you go from a positive to a negative with the *or*.

Likewise, if the question asks you what the minimum is in group A, for example, count how many *or* pairs you have, as one of those variables must always be in. So, if you have two "or pair" rules, that's a minimum of two variables that must always be in. On the other hand, if negative to positive (e.g., if Z then not W; if W then not Z), the group now is reduced by one. Basically, you can never have ZW together. One of these variables now must be out. This is indicated by the "not both" in the grouping games.

For example, either X or Y is in group A, but not both (their enemies). If you're asked which of the following "Must Be False," look to see which rule doesn't have a floater in it and test it. Remember: a floater doesn't have a restriction on it, so it cannot be true or false. So if a non-floater doesn't work out, then that answer choice Must Be False.

- Tips: Since it's formal logic, there will be very little deductions up front. Quickly write rules, contrapose, and link up duplicate entities to form a chain. If you don't have any overlap of rules, move on to the questions fast since the questions are going to be all "if-then" questions. Also think about multiple sketches; multiple sketches are good when you have one variable doing two different tasks. For example, if the rule says "if M in 3rd, then T in Team A" and "if M not in 3rd, then Z in team B," draw both possibilities for M. When you see an MBT question, draw more sketches and see what MBT in both. Also, there are some common rules to understand (assuming only two positions:

211

one and two) of which you may want to draw multiple sketches. For example, if the rule states "If ~ G1, then W1":
- First Possibility: G2 (i.e. ~ G1), W1 (original rule)
- Second Possibility: W2, G1 (i.e. ~ G2; contrapositive)
- Third Possibility: W1, G1 (The necessary conditions for both are okay.)
- Note: Because there are only two slots (1 and 2) this creates a bi-conditional rule (i.e., they are both in or both out); If G1, then W1 if but only if W1, G1.
  - This means they are best friends (BFFs). G1 & W1 are both in or both out (BFFs). This creates a GW block or not-GW block
- <u>Sketch:</u> Use a T-chart, or simply circle and dash who's in and who's out. If you don't circle or dash, then they can be either in or out; you don't know.
  - ABCDE (entities: select 4/5)
  - In | Out
  - _ _ _ _ | _

Question Strategy:
1. Do rule elimination first.
2. Do "if/CBT questions" second.
3. Do if MBT/MBF third. (Do sub-game boards to see all options.)
4. Do MBT/MBF open-ended fourth. (Look at other sub-game boards to eliminate answers.) Note: here you will have to test each answer choice. Don't start with any floaters (i.e., no rules mention the floater entity, so it can't be a "must be" by default).

APPENDIX E: LOGIC-GAMES HOMEWORK—PRACTICE DRILLS BY QUESTION TYPE

5. Skip rule substitution questions, if running out of time.
6. If you see "complete determined question," test the entity not mentioned in the rules (i.e., the floater) first. Also test the most restricted rule first.
7. If you see "complete and accurate list" it's like a rule-elimination question. Test each rule and eliminate.

Logic Games Distribution Prep Test Homework:
2, 3, 6, 7, 9, 11, 12, 13, 14, 17, 18, 19, 21, 22, 24, **26, 27,** 29, 34, 37, 38, 41, **44,** 49, **52, 53,** 61, 63, **66,** 68, 69, 71, 72, 73, 75 February 97, C.

Notes with Distribution:

- Entities: two sets
- Action: Group bigger into smaller (players into teams); assign each person to a zone
- Hints to Know Game Type: *assign to exactly one, evaluated by one, exactly six workers into two cars, each team gets at least one player, sort into groups*
- Think About: Are there any groups that can be empty? How big are the groups? What are the group's limitations? Who's NOT selected for the group? A very common rule will have an *or* in it, indicating that either one or the other is in (maybe both). For example, if X or Y is in group A that means: if Not X then Y is in; if not Y, then X is in. This means that group A cannot be empty; at least one must be in. On the other hand, with a "not both" rule: if Z then not W; if W then not Z. Now the group is reduced by one. Basically you can never have ZW together.

- So, when a rule says "P or T, but not both," write "never PT" or "either P/T" in that specific group. Next, think about the numbers and the possibilities. Draw different sketches early to see all possibilities and determine what Must Be True and False from what Could Be True and False. However, if there are more than two sketches that can be drawn (i.e., tons of possibilities), don't waste your time and jump into the questions. Also, after you write the rules, ask what the flip side is. For example, if a rule says "K can't be in O" (and there's only one other spot for it W), then write down that K must be in W.
- <u>Tips:</u> Entities are fixed, unlike in matching games. Once placed they cannot move around. To handle "if" questions, ask if your rules were triggered or failed. If a question makes the sufficient condition of a rule fail, then the rule doesn't exist anymore. In contrast, if the rule makes a necessary condition fail, then the sufficient condition fails (i.e., it's testing the contrapositive). In other words, if the rule was "if K in 3 then W in 4" and the question put W in 5, it failed the necessary condition so the sufficient condition can't be in 3 (i.e., K must be somewhere else). This is the contrapositive being triggered.
- Finally, for "completely determined questions," go through each answer choice and see which game board the answer choice corresponds to. If two out of three game boards don't mention the rule but the third game board does, then that makes it completely determined and that is the correct answer.
- <u>Sketch:</u> Use tables with headers and columns.

APPENDIX E: LOGIC-GAMES HOMEWORK—PRACTICE DRILLS BY QUESTION TYPE

Question Strategy:
1. Do rule elimination first.
2. Do "if/CBT questions" second.
3. Do if MBT/MBF third. (Do sub-game boards to see all options.)
4. Do MBT/MBF open-ended fourth. (Look at other sub-game boards to eliminate answers.) Note: here you will have to test each answer choice. Don't start with any floaters (i.e., no rules mention the floater entity so it can't be a "must be" by default).
5. Skip rule-substitution questions, if running out of time.
6. If you see a "complete determined question," test the entity not mentioned in the rules (i.e., the floater) first. Also, test the most restricted rule first.
7. If you see "complete and accurate list" it's like a rule-elimination question. Test each rule and eliminate.

Logic Games Matching Prep Test Homework:
1, 3, 4, 5, 6, 7, 8, 9, 10, 12, 14, 16, 17, 21, 22, 27, 28, 29, 30, 33, 34, 35, 37, 39, 42, 43, 44, **45, 46**, 47, **48,** 51, 56, 57, 62, 64, 67, 68, 73 June 2007, C, **77.**

Notes with Matching:
- Entities: two sets
- Action: Match both entities together (e.g., colors to cars).
- Hints to Know Game Type: *match*, *select*, or if it says "at least one," you know that entities are floating around
- Think About: Do all entities have to be used? Think about the numbers. For example, if six cars need to be matched,

it can be 3:2:1 or 2:2:2. Draw out your options early to see all possibilities. When reading the game, if you realize that you have to put five entities into nine slots, for example, and the entities have to repeat, then use a chart for the sketch.
- <u>Tips:</u> Big points surround numbers in the game. Break up into as many options as possible and start plugging in the charts to see what Must Be True and Could Be True.
- <u>Sketch:</u> Use tables with headers and columns. Use ellipses (. . .), as entities can float around.

Question Strategy:
1. Do rule elimination first.
2. Do "if/CBT" questions" second.
3. Do if MBT/MBF third. (Do sub-game boards to see all options.)
4. Do MBT/MBF open-ended fourth. (Look at other sub-game boards to eliminate answers). Note: here you will have to test each answer choice. Don't start with any floaters (i.e., no rules mention the floater entity, so it can't be a "must be" by default).
5. Skip "rule-substitution questions," if running out of time.
6. If you see "complete determined questions," test the entity not mentioned in the rules (i.e., the floater) first. Also, test the most restricted rule first.
8. If you see "complete and accurate list," it's like a rule-elimination question. Test each rule and eliminate.

APPENDIX F: Reading-Comp Question Identification Types

Big Picture (too detailed or narrow in focus is wrong)

- Main idea of passage?
- Primary purpose of the passage is?
- Best describes the organization of the passage?
- Which best describes the passage as a whole?
- Which most accurately describes the author's attitude towards?
- Which one of the following best states the main conclusion of the passage?
- The passage as a whole can be described as?

Detail (restatement of text in a summary form; too broad an answer choice is wrong)

- According to the information in the passage . . .
- Which one of the following does the passage mention?

- Author explicitly claims that which one of the following . . .
- Which one of the following most accurately expresses the meaning of X?
- Which one of the following is mentioned in the passage as a reason why X happened?

Inference (must put your finger on the line in the passage that supports the answer choice; extreme answers are wrong)

- Author mentions X most probably to?
- Author of the passage would most likely agree with?
- Which one of the following can be inferred from the passage?
- It can be inferred from the passage that the author would be most likely to agree with?
- Which one of the following most characterizes the author's view regarding . . . ?
- Which X would not cover in paragraph three?
- The passage suggests that the type of?
- Author quotes X in line 16 primarily in order to?
- The passage supports each of the following except?
- The author implies that . . .
- The passage suggests that which one of the following is true?

APPENDIX F: READING-COMP QUESTION IDENTIFICATION TYPES

Logical-reasoning questions (all about "why" the author mentioned; anything about details of "the what" is wrong)

- Which one of the following could replace the term X for Y?
- Which one of the following could most logically be added to the end?
- Which one of the following underlies the author's argument in the third paragraph?
- Which one of the following principles . . . ?
- Which one of the following is most analogous to lines 13-15?
- The author's argument in lines 20-25 would be most weakened if which one of the following were true?
- The function of paragraph X is . . . ?

APPENDIX G: Reading-Comp Structure Patterns

Structure is key when it comes to answering the big-picture questions. Below are two main types of passages: the ones that argue something, and the ones that explain something. Remember: for every paragraph you read, "push up" and connect it to the main point and ask how it relates to the author's purpose. This will really "lock in" each paragraph to the main point of the passage as a whole. To help you see the relationships, circle or box the following type of keywords and turning points (i.e., hard breaks) to help you identify the common reading comprehension structures below:

- **Modifiers/Adjectives:** *astonishing* computer, *outstanding* impact, *strong* x, *unfair* advantage etc.
- **Something needed:** *must, require*
- **Opinions:** *best represents, negative effect, goes against, landmark, should, formidable,* etc.
- **Qualifiers:** *more likely, little,* etc.

APPENDIX G: READING-COMP STRUCTURE PATTERNS

- **Subject/Nouns:** what's it about (names, candidates)
- **Predicate/Verbs:** *charged, advocated,* etc.
- **Background info before turning point:** *but, although, however, some people say*

"Explain" Passage Structures
1. Event introduced; first response to it discussed; second response to it described.
2. Old theory, support for new theory, details of support, possible application of new theory.
3. Introduce topic such as poetry; introduce poem that is popular at the time; elaborate on how it's different from the rest.
4. Identification of a movement, potential issues with the movement, achievements of the movement.
5. Introduce new theory; discuss background on what led to it; provide more research on components within it.
6. Introduce a theory and gives an example; discuss three advantages of it; provide proof from experiments; provide more proof from field tests.
7. Background on topic, challenge with researching it, the impact today.
8. Phenomenon introduced, two-part description of it, details of each explained.
9. Introduce phenomenon; author discusses failed early attempts to mitigate; author introduces another perspective.
10. Introduction of two-part thesis; first part discussed; second part discussed.

11. Phenomenon is introduced and explanation is offered, reasons against, support for it, further support for it.
12. Advantage of X, disadvantage of X, ways to mitigate the disadvantage.

"Argue" Passage Structures
1. Main point/thesis, support, support, summary of main point.
2. Problem; three possible solutions; three criticisms; new, fourth solution introduced.
3. Introduces shift in laws from A to B; author presents viewpoint; author introduces historical views and limitations (A); author argues for his approach (B).
4. Intro to old view and new view; discussion of new view by analogy; analogy elaborated; analogy taken to an extreme; extreme compared to non-extreme analogy; author's main point at end.
5. Two positions in a debate; author presents A and challenges it; argues for B.
6. Description of plan, arguments for and against it, author chooses a side.
7. Introduce viewpoint A; introduce viewpoint B; knock down B and introduce author's viewpoint, C; compare C to A and show how it's better.
8. Main point/thesis is introduced comparing A and B (A>B), support for A (i.e., why B is bad), more support (why A is good).
9. Introduce two systems (A & B), support for A, support of B>A.

APPENDIX G: READING-COMP STRUCTURE PATTERNS

10. Criticism of phenomenon argued for, then challenged; supporting examples; how phenomenon works and how it is good are explained.
11. Introduce topic; highlight recent need for it; discuss effects of implementing it.
12. Author criticism of phenomenon; explanation of criticism; example of criticism; recap summary of criticism.
13. Phenomenon introduced; details about the style explained; question posed as to how phenomenon was successful; author's main point praising phenomenon and its impact.
14. Introduce old phenomenon; introduce new phenomenon; provide examples in support of new one; provide one example of old phenomenon being bad.
15. Background information; problem; two possible solutions by X; critics negate solutions; third, better solution; critics negate better solution; impact on problem applied to the world; author's solution and what is needed to implement.

APPENDIX H: 25 Signs You're Ready to Sit and "Write" the LSAT

1. You go from wanting to just get into law school to getting some scholarship money to wanting to get a perfect score of 180.
2. You read road signs and think of contrapositives.
3. You point out flaws with people's arguments or attack their assumptions.
4. You actually think before you use the words "must/need" instead of "could/will."
5. You notice equivocation being used in your favorite songs.
6. You feel empowered when skipping a problem under timed conditions (as opposed to being anxious or nervous).
7. You are able to complete three reading-comprehension passages, three logic games, and at least 18 questions on logical reasoning consistently under timed conditions.

APPENDIX H: 25 SIGNS YOU'RE READY TO SIT AND "WRITE" THE LSAT

8. You underline each word that makes the wrong answer choice incorrect.
9. You pay attention to every word as if it's under a magnifying glass.
10. You could regurgitate strategy by question type if someone woke you up from deep sleep at 3 a.m. (e.g., sufficient assumption versus necessary assumption).
11. You go from hating logic games to loving them and thinking they serve as a nice breather from the rest of the sections.
12. You try to become a test-writer by turning questions into other type of questions. For example, you swap out keywords to turn strengthening questions into weakening questions.
13. You can predict which section you are about to do by looking at the number of questions it has (e.g., 27 questions is reading comprehension, or 23 in logic games).
14. You try to fit every English sentence into a sufficient versus necessary condition.
15. You start focusing on the hardest questions, games, and passages first instead of last.
16. You start looking up state statutes and municipality ordinances.
17. You go from wanting to know how many correct questions you got (e.g., 15 or 18 right) to wanting to know how many questions you missed (e.g., minus three, minus five) after a Prep Test.

18. You notice how each section interrelates with the others. For example, how inference questions in logical reasoning are "mini logic games" in which you need to find what Must Be True and eliminate Could Be False answer choices.
19. You compare and contrast trends from decades of Prep Tests. For example, Prep Tests in the sixties tested flaws more, versus those in the 70s, which tested principle questions more.
20. You know every ratio that can impact your score. For example, how many questions you attempted/how many you got correct or exactly how many correct you need to bubble in to get a 150, etc.
21. You never want to use a *most, all,* or *none* statement again.
22. You turn every wrong answer choice into a correct answer choice.
23. You realize common wrong-answer traps are Could Be True or Could Be False or require you to make an unreasonable assumption.
24. You score "your best" on the actual LSAT and want to redo it to try to beat it.
25. You write a book about it. ☺

APPENDIX I: Common Wrong-Answer-Choice Traps in Logical Reasoning

After doing almost every single logical-reasoning question from Prep Tests 1-77, I compiled a list of common incorrect-answer traps. Every answer choice must be supported 100 percent of the time. If there is any doubt (i.e., it Could Be True or Could Be False), it's more than likely wrong.

- Extreme answer choices. Anything that says *all, none, most, primarily, only, only if, essential,* etc.
- CBT/CBF answer choices. For example:
  - Stimulus talks about smoking and answer choice mentions not smoking.
  - Stimulus discusses one breed of dogs and answer choice mentions other breeds of dogs.
  - Stimulus discusses costs and answer choice mentions profit.
  - Any new information or term introduced out of nowhere, such as "other XYZ" (e.g., "running" in

stimulus but answer choice discusses certain types of running, like marathon running).
- Deductions made from some statements or some statements' contrapositives (both Must Be False). For example: some people do X in the stimulus but the answer choice says that no people do X. (Only categorical statements have contrapositives.)
- Relative comparison answer choice that is irrelevant to stimulus. Any answer choice that has X as *more, less, other, greater than* Y, but the stimulus doesn't mention one of the two variables.
- Restatement of premises (including in the contrapositive). This is common on assumption questions since assumptions, by definition, are unstated.
- Any unreasonable assumptions required to be made. This is found in harder logical-reasoning questions where you are required to compare assumptions in the answer choices. The more reasonable the assumption between the two is correct.

APPENDIX J: Acceptance Letters

The law school admissions game is another book in itself. It is probably the second most stressful time of your pre-law school period after taking the LSAT and receiving your score. If you go on lawschoolnumbers.com, you will see a self-reporting system of other student's acceptance, rejected, and waitlisted status. Some may have scored lower than you, and some may have scored higher. All you can do is play the cards that you were dealt based on your UGPA and LSAT score.

My advice is to apply early. If you want to start in the fall, then send applications around November of the previous year and be prepared to write the October LSAT. Some schools won't send your application to their committee for review if they see you have another scheduled LSAT (e.g. in December or February). If you get in great; if you get waitlisted, then re-schedule to take the LSAT again (December or February) and score higher so you can use this new score to get bumped off the waitlist and become accepted.

Also, during the waitlist period visit the school and meet

the admissions committee. Remember names, faces, and send a follow-up thank you card and letters of intent. Tell them your willing to start in the summer if you have to. They tend to give admissions for those that want to be there and show interest and appreciate the opportunity. Wouldn't you? Also, every year all the schools get together to meet at the "law school forum." Go to this event (usually at a hotel somewhere) and get as many application "waiver codes" as you can. If you don't get a waiver code there, then email the school asking for one. The more applications you can send out the better your chances of getting accepted or put on the waitlist. If you get on 20-waitlists for example, you have time to "work" your top school choices (visiting, calling, emailing, etc.). Finally, if you get rejected, then it's all right; just charge it to the game.

Usually, an accepted status is followed up by a phone call from the school congratulating you. A waitlist (or rejection) is usually an email. Save the postage right? If your scores are high, you have leverage. The first scholarship offer they give you counter back and see if they can give you more (use evidence of another school's offering). It's all business at the end of the day; they need your stats to pump up their law school rankings.

Choosing a school and location is going to be a very tough decision. You have to balance scholarship offers versus ranking status and location. If you're thinking about going to an unranked school (tier four) with the intent of "transferring up" to a ranked school, it's likely not to happen. Everyone is in your same boat with the same game plan. Transfers are usually the top 10% of the class. Just remember, many high scorers choose lower ranked schools because they might have received a full ride. Therefore, these students could be your competition.

Attached are the several accepted and waitlisted letters I received. Being close to the middle of the LSAT bell curve, I, unfortunately, got placed on many wait lists. If I had read this one Appendix before applying my outcome could have been different. Regardless, it sure feels great to work so hard and see so many acceptance letters with scholarship offers. So, work hard on the LSAT, apply early, and work the waitlist by doing a re-take of the LSAT and visiting the schools. Good luck and let me know where you get into (@shahofmiami)!

LSAT NECESSARY: An LSAT Prep Test Guide for the Non-logical Thinker

INDIANA UNIVERSITY
MAURER SCHOOL OF LAW
Bloomington

April 4, 2016

aarambh shah

Dear Mr. shah:

Congratulations! On behalf of the faculty at Indiana University Maurer School of Law, it is my pleasure to inform you that you have been admitted to the Indiana Law Class of 2019, with studies commencing in August of 2016. Your acceptance to one of the nation's oldest, most prestigious law schools is an affirmation of our confidence in your intellectual capacity to succeed in a demanding course of study and in your potential to make substantive contributions to the Indiana Law community, both as a student and as a proud graduate.

I am also pleased to inform you that you have been selected to receive a renewable ████ scholarship (based on nonresident status) which will total ████ **over three years**, is strictly merit-based and not dependent upon any showing of financial need. The award is renewable contingent upon your maintaining satisfactory progress at the end of your first year (a 2.3 or higher) as well as each subsequent semester thereafter and not being disciplined for misconduct.

At Indiana Law, where the student-to-faculty ratio is less than nine-to-one, you will have an incredible opportunity to work closely with our nationally renowned faculty to advance knowledge and to promote our tradition of excellence in the practice of law and service to others. You will be given access to Indiana University's other top-ranked programs — including the School of Public and Environmental Affairs, the Kelley School of Business, and the School of Global and International Affairs, to name a few. And as a student here, you will benefit from an international network of more than 12,000 alumni, and an integrated approach to career services and professional development. Indiana Law is a school with national prominence, and our graduates go on to practice throughout the country and all over the world.

To secure your place in the Class of 2019, please complete the enclosed confirmation form, and return it to lawadmis@indiana.edu no later than **April 22, 2016**. Unlike many law schools, we do not require a seat deposit. Our tradition is to accept your word as an aspirant to the legal profession.

An admitted student webpage summarizing the tasks related to enrolling at Indiana Law this fall has been posted at ████. We encourage you to use this page as your resource for information about financial aid, campus visits, housing, and our **Summer Start program**. For th████

We would be honored to have you join us in Bloomington for a legal education amidst one of the most beautiful university campuses in the United States, and become part of this law school's venerable legacy of producing leaders of the bar, government, and private sector. If you have any questions or would like to visit Indiana Law, please feel free to call 812-855-4765 or send an email to lawadmis@indiana.edu at any time.

Sincerely,

Greg Canada
Assistant Dean of Admissions

Admissions Office Baier Hall 211 S. Indiana Avenue Bloomington, IN 47405-7001 (812) 855-4765 lawadmis@indiana.edu www.law.indiana.edu

APPENDIX J: ACCEPTANCE LETTERS

UNIVERSITY OF ILLINOIS
AT URBANA-CHAMPAIGN

College of Law

Office of Admissions and Financial Aid
201 Law Building
504 East Pennsylvania Avenue
Champaign, IL 61820

June 27, 2016

Mr. Aarambh M. Shah

Dear Aarambh:

    Congratulations! On behalf of the entire Illinois Law community, I am delighted to offer you admission to the Class of 2019 at the University of Illinois College of Law. Moreover, in recognition of your exceptional academic and personal accomplishments, we will award you, upon matriculation, a tuition scholarship in the amount of ███████ per year. Your tuition and scholarship are subject to the *Illinois Guarantee* – we guarantee that your law tuition will not increase during the three years you are a student here and that your scholarship will be renewed at the previously mentioned level for each semester that you are enrolled as a full-time student at the College of Law. Enclosed please find more detail regarding your scholarship. We do not condition your scholarship renewal on any minimum GPA or other academic performance criteria.

    Gaining admission to Illinois Law is an accomplishment of which you should be enormously proud. We receive applications from some of the brightest, hardest-working and most accomplished law school applicants anywhere. To have been selected from among such a distinguished group is a testament to your tremendous potential as a law student and as an attorney.

DEPOSITS:

    In order to accept this offer of admission, you are required to pay one (1) tuition deposit. The schedule below details the one (1) tuition deposit which will be credited to your Fall 2016 tuition and fees. The deposit is non-refundable in the event that you do not enroll.

- Deposit of $500, due no later than Friday, July 8, 2016

    You may pay the deposit online by logging into the Admitted Student site (user name: ███████ 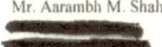 at ███████████████████████████████ or you may mail a check to the Office of Admissions. If you would like to pay both deposits at once, you are welcome to do so.

telephone 217-244-6415 • *fax* 217-244-1478

LSAT NECESSARY: An LSAT Prep Test Guide for the Non-logical Thinker

Mr. Aarambh M. Shah
June 27, 2016
Page 2

VISITING CAMPUS:

You are also welcome to visit the College of Law on your own. Please call the Office of Admissions and Financial Aid at 217.244.6415 to schedule an individual visit. Visits can include a tour of the law school and a meeting with an admissions counselor. Travel assistance is also available for individual visits. We are excited to meet you!

TRANSCRIPTS:

The American Bar Association (ABA) requires matriculants to ABA-approved law schools to have earned at least a bachelor's degree prior to beginning classes. Accordingly, please arrange for one (1) official transcript to be sent from your degree-granting undergraduate institution directly to the Office of Admissions and Financial Aid at the College of Law. The transcript must indicate conferral of a bachelor's degree and must be **received prior to August 1, 2016.** Please note: transcripts issued to students or submitted via the LSDAS are not official and do not satisfy this requirement.

ADDITIONAL INFORMATION:

Please keep this letter for your reference in the coming months. We have enclosed information we hope you will find useful. You can find much more information about Illinois Law on our website - www.law.illinois.edu - including profiles of our distinguished professors, descriptions of our academic and clinical programs, and news about our impressive alumni. The website also includes an admitted student-only section (user name: ███████████████ which includes resources that we hope confirm that Illinois Law is the right school for you. At any time, please feel welcome to contact anyone in the Office of Admissions and Financial Aid with questions or concerns.

Once again, congratulations on your well-deserved offer of admission. Since 1897, the University of Illinois College of Law has produced some of the finest attorneys, judges, business persons, and advocates in this nation. We hope you will choose to further their legacy and begin your own successful career at Illinois Law!

Sincerely,

Rebecca Ray
Assistant Dean for Admissions
and Financial Aid

Enclosures

APPENDIX J: ACCEPTANCE LETTERS

DEPAUL
UNIVERSITY

April 21, 2016

College of Law
Office of Admission
25 East Jackson Boulevard
Chicago, Illinois 60604-2287
312/362-6831
FAX: 312/362-5280

Aarambh Shah

Dear Mr. Shah:

I am delighted to inform you that the Admissions Committee, having reviewed and evaluated your academic accomplishments, personal achievements and potential for legal studies, has accepted you for admission to the College of Law.

Through your academic achievement, aptitude and strength of personal qualities, you have demonstrated a fine potential for legal studies and service to the legal profession. I commend you, Aarambh, on such noteworthy qualifications and enthusiastically join the Admissions Committee in wishing you every success. Welcome to the DePaul community and to the full-time day program Class of 2019!

I am also delighted to inform you that, in recognition of your achievements, personal qualities, and potential to contribute to the DePaul community, the College of Law will award you a ███ Scholarship in the total amount of $███. The ███ Scholarship will be applied toward tuition in the amount of $███ for the 2016-2017 academic year. This award is guaranteed in the same amount for your two remaining academic years provided that you are enrolled as a full-time student. There is no GPA requirement to renew this award.

During the next several weeks, you will be devoting a good deal of time to assessing the criteria that you value in a law school. I encourage you at any time to contact the Office of Admissions. We understand that selecting a law school involves a number of considerations and commitments, both on a professional and a personal level. We promise to do our best in serving your needs and I invite you to contact me directly by email at ███████████. You may also contact our Assistant Director of Admissions, Elisa Correa by email at ███████████ or by telephone at ███████.

As you prepare to select a law school, I encourage you to again review and reaffirm your reasons for ultimately seeking a career in law and for considering DePaul.

A good law school must provide a mix of professional skills training, traditional substantive law subjects and theoretical courses to stretch the minds of law students. It must also provide a cooperative and supportive environment that will instill the professional values that are important to all. I believe DePaul creates that kind of community.

DePaul faculty members are a nationally prominent community of teachers and legal scholars who place the highest priority on programs of instruction and learning. They are accessible, approachable and deeply committed to their students. Evaluations of faculty scholarship have also placed DePaul very high. Our faculty members are actively engaged in discovering how the law might be both improved and better understood. The faculty support seven student-edited journals and digests, as well as fourteen research centers and institutes.

LSAT NECESSARY: An LSAT Prep Test Guide for the Non-logical Thinker

Aarambh Shah
April 21, 2016
Page two

In summary, I invite you to come to DePaul because of the opportunities and challenges we offer. I invite you to become part of an institution with a tradition of educating lawyers who are unrivaled with respect to the positions of leadership they hold in law firms, corporations, government agencies and in the judiciary. Enter DePaul prepared to drive yourself to your best efforts; enter prepared to develop your talents to the fullest.

I hope DePaul is your choice, and I look forward to welcoming you on Wednesday, August 17 for New Student Orientation & Classes. Our Orientation is a special and required two-day program designed to acquaint you with our first-year program of study and with your professors, classmates and the staff. Some classes begin during Orientation.

To confirm your acceptance and to hold your seat in the entering class, you must forward in a timely manner a total tuition deposit of six-hundred dollars, which may be paid in two equal installments of three-hundred dollars. Your tuition deposit is non-refundable and will be applied toward your tuition for the Fall Semester. Please use the enclosed envelope to forward your deposit. Please ensure the envelope is received in the Office of Admissions on or before Monday, May 16, 2016. Please print your name, mailing address, and either Social Security Number or LSAC account number on the inside of the envelope. In the alternative, you may pay your tuition deposit online through Campus Connection at ▓▓▓▓▓▓▓▓▓▓▓▓▓▓▓. Your DePaul Campus Connection username and password is enclosed.

Should you elect to pay the tuition deposit in two installments, the second deposit must be received in the Office of Admissions on or before Wednesday, June 15, 2016. Should you fail to forward these deposit installments by the required dates, you may lose your seat. To accept your scholarship award, please sign and submit the enclosed 2016-2017 ▓▓▓▓ Scholarship Award Form, along with your tuition deposit, to the Office of Admissions by using the enclosed envelope. In the alternative, you may sign, scan and send an electronic copy of the signed form by email to ▓▓▓▓▓▓▓▓▓▓▓ or by fax to (312) 362-5280.

The American Bar Association requires that the law school in which you enroll have an official and final copy of your undergraduate transcript that posts your undergraduate degree. If you submitted your undergraduate college transcript to LSAC prior to having completed your degree, you must request that your university send another official transcript to LSAC which shows that your undergraduate degree was completed. LSAC will update your JD CAS report with your final transcript and verify conferral of your baccalaureate degree.

Once again, I commend you on your accomplishments and congratulate you on your admission to the full-time day program. You join a distinguished DePaul community of students, scholars, professors and alumni. I am confident that you will find DePaul College of Law and the city of Chicago to be stimulating settings in which to achieve your academic, professional and personal goals.

Sincerely,

Stephanie Basañez Gunn
Director of Admissions

Enclosures

APPENDIX J: ACCEPTANCE LETTERS

Santa Clara University

April 19, 2016

Aarambh Shah

Dear Mr. Shah:

Congratulations! I am pleased to inform you that you have been admitted as a full-time student in the School of Law beginning in the fall 2016 semester. The School of Law's Committee on Admissions is impressed with your potential as a law student and a prospective member of the legal profession. We are extremely proud of our students and alumni and believe you have the credentials and ambition to join this community.

Since 1911, the School of Law has been educating lawyers with uncompromising standards of excellence and the potential for achievement as community leaders. As a member of our community, you will be joining the ranks of many accomplished men and women. As a student at Santa Clara Law, you will have an opportunity to study with a distinguished faculty of national and international reputation. You will also find what sets Santa Clara Law apart from other law schools - a sense of community, a culture of support for personal and professional growth, and a mutual respect among students, faculty, and staff. I am confident that you will find your experience here academically and professionally rewarding.

I encourage you to learn more about Santa Clara Law by visiting our campus and speaking with our students, faculty, and staff. Please do not hesitate to call our Admissions Office to plan your visit. The Admissions staff will assist you with any questions you have as you prepare to embark on your legal studies.

To affirm your commitment to Santa Clara Law and reserve your place in the class, please send a nonrefundable seat deposit of $250.00 to the Office of Admissions by May 15, 2016. This is a firm date by which the deposit must be received, not postmarked, or your seat in the class will be forfeited. A second deposit of $550.00 will be due by June 1. These deposits will be credited toward your fall tuition.

We are excited about your admission to Santa Clara Law and I look forward to meeting you during a campus visit or at a new student event. Once again, congratulations on your fine achievements, and welcome to the Santa Clara Law community.

Sincerely,

Nanette Cannon
Director of Admissions

Enclosures

School of Law, Admissions Office / Financial Aid
500 El Camino Real, Santa Clara, California 95053-0435
408-554-5048 FAX 408-554-7897 http://law.scu.edu

LSAT NECESSARY: An LSAT Prep Test Guide for the Non-logical Thinker

OFFICE OF ADMISSIONS AND FINANCIAL AID

April 21, 2016

Aarambh M. Shah

Dear Aarambh,

It is my pleasure to inform you that you have been accepted for admission to Mercer University School of Law as a member of the 2016 entering class. All of us at Mercer Law consider it an honor to be part of your journey to becoming a Mercer lawyer. You have much to look forward to in your legal education and beyond, and we are excited about being a part of that.

If you have not yet visited the Law School, I invite you to do so. You may attend a first year class, have a tour, and meet members of the Mercer Law community. This is a great opportunity to experience what distinguishes Mercer from other law schools- first year class sections of 25 students, individualized feedback from professors, and a supportive environment between students, faculty, and staff.

You are required to submit a $500.00 seat deposit no later than May 6, 2016. This deposit is non-refundable but will be applied to your fall 2016 tuition. If you wish to pay by credit card you may pay online at ▓▓▓▓▓▓▓▓▓▓▓▓▓▓▓▓▓▓▓▓. If you wish to pay by check or money order, please make payable to Mercer University and include your LSAC account number. Failure to meet the seat deposit deadlines will result in the forfeiture of your place in the first-year class.

Please feel free to contact us with questions or concerns by calling 478-301-2605 or email us at admissions@law.mercer.edu.

I look forward to welcoming you to the Class of 2019!

Sincerely,

Marilyn E. Sutton
Assistant Dean of Admissions and Financial Aid

Congratulations!

MERCER UNIVERSITY | WALTER F. GEORGE SCHOOL OF LAW
1021 Georgia Avenue | Macon, GA 31207 | law.mercer.edu | 1-800-342-0841 Inside GA and 1-800-637-2378 Outside GA
Financial Aid (478) 301-2147 | Admissions (478) 301-2605

APPENDIX J: ACCEPTANCE LETTERS

March 2, 2016

Mr. Aarambh Shah

Dear Mr. Shah:

Congratulations again on your admission to Akron Law. Our Admissions Committee was very impressed with your outstanding achievements and exceptional academic record. In recognition of your remarkable qualifications, as well as your strong potential for success, The University of Akron School of Law Admissions Committee has selected you to receive a scholarship in the amount of ▓▓▓▓ for the **Full-Time** 2016-2017 academic year. **Congratulations!**

Your scholarship is an annual, renewable scholarship that will be divided evenly between the spring and fall semester of each academic year. Please also note that all Akron Law Scholarships are guaranteed for your entire law school career – no stipulations, no strings attached. As long as you are not academically dismissed from law school, the scholarship will be renewed for the entire duration of your enrollment here at Akron Law, meaning that the total value of the scholarship over the course of your **Full-Time** program is ▓▓▓▓.

As you compare our scholarship offer to offers from other law schools, please keep in mind that while other schools might also offer you a scholarship, those other schools often require you to maintain a certain minimum GPA to renew your scholarship. The required GPA may only be achieved by 25-30% of the first year class. In contrast to these schools, Akron Law scholarships are guaranteed for your entire time at Akron Law. We view this scholarship offer as an investment in your education and in your future, which is why we simply ask that you maintain good academic standing in order to renew it.

To accept and reserve your scholarship, you must submit your **$350 seat deposit** by **9 am on Friday, April 15, 2016**. Failure to submit your seat deposit by this deadline will result in the loss of your scholarship.

At Akron Law, we strive to make a legal education financially realistic for all admitted applicants. In addition to the excellent legal education that you will receive here, the high degree of personal attention we offer to our admitted and enrolled students is emblematic of the value we place upon all members of our community.

The Akron Law faculty and staff look forward to welcoming you. In the meantime, please contact me if you have any questions. Again, congratulations on your admission and on your scholarship. We are certain that Akron Law will be the beginning of a great legal career for you.

Sincerely,

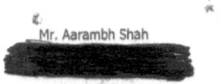

Barbara C. Weinzierl
Assistant Dean for Admissions and Strategic Initiatives

School of Law
Akron, OH 44325-2901
330-972-7331 • 330-258-2343 Fax

LSAT NECESSARY: An LSAT Prep Test Guide for the Non-logical Thinker

MITCHELL HAMLINE
School of Law

Aarambh Shah

Dear Aram,

Welcome! You have been admitted to the fall 2016 inaugural class at Mitchell Hamline School of Law as a Full Time student. We are delighted to offer you a ___% Tuition Scholarship.

Achieve your goals. Your success is our number one priority. Each student is treated as an individual. Our personalized approach will help you to meet your educational and professional goals, including:

- **Experiential Progression.** Guaranteed experiential opportunities even in your first year.
- **Academic Success.** Individual tutoring and skills workshops included at no additional cost.
- **Career Development.** You will have a designated career advisor dedicated to your future.
- **Alumni Mentors.** 19,000 alumni committed to connecting you to the legal community.

A distinct advantage. As a member of Mitchell Hamline's inaugural class, you will benefit from our combined 150 years of practical, problem-solving legal education. Mitchell Hamline's innovative approach to legal education makes it a leader in meeting the needs of the ever-evolving legal marketplace.

Meet your faculty ambassador. A unique benefit of Mitchell Hamline is our faculty ambassador program. Each incoming student is paired with a professor who provides personalized guidance to demystify the law school experience, answer your questions, and support your success. Your faculty ambassador is Prof. **Marie Failinger**. Expect to receive an email soon. However, you can feel free to reach out a___

Secure your seat. To accept your offer, a $500 non-refundable tuition deposit and Secure your Seat form is due by April 15, 2016. You can pay your deposit online through our Admitted Student website or by check.

Congratulations on your admission and scholarship! I am happy to discuss your offer with you. Please feel free to be in contact with me directly a___ or 651-290-6434.

Warm regards,

Emily M. Dunsworth
Assistant Dean of Admissions

Congrats, Aram! We hope you join us at MHSL this fall!

APPENDIX J: ACCEPTANCE LETTERS

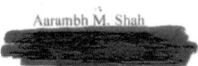

School of Law
Office of Admissions

February 11, 2016

Aarambh M. Shah

Dear Aarambh:

Congratulations! I am extremely pleased to inform you of your acceptance in the JD program at Howard University School of Law for fall 2016. You are one in a select group of academically gifted students offered the opportunity to share the rich traditions, inviting community and educational opportunities that are cornerstones of the Howard University experience.

Here at Howard, you will join an illustrious tradition of scholarship and unparalleled commitment to the pursuit of excellence. The faculty, students, and administration enthusiastically look forward to the start of your matriculation in the fall of 2016. We are confident that your dedication to scholarship will make you a worthy candidate to accept and carry the torch now passed to a new generation of the Howard University School of Law.

The fall semester begins in **August 2016** for all first-year students. Please pay attention to the **enclosed Fact Sheet** as it advises you of important business matters and deadlines.

We will communicate throughout the process via email. Please insure the email address you provided on your application is an address you check on a consistent basis. Please add Howard University School of Law to a safe list to insure vital information does not end up in a junk mail folder. Also we recommend you visit the status checker attached to your file on a consistent basis for real time updates to your admissions status.

If you are disabled as defined in the American with Disabilities Act, and you need accommodation, please inform Adrienne Packard, Director of Student Affairs at 202-806-8006 or promptly of this need.

Sincerely,

Reginald McGahee
Associate Dean of Student Affairs and Admissions

2900 Van Ness Street, NW
Washington, DC 20008

Telephone (202) 806 8008/09
Facsimile (202) 806 8162
www.howard.edu

School of Law

March 9, 2016

Mr. Aarambh M. Shah

Dear Mr. Shah:

Thank you for your patience and continued interest in Georgia Law. The Admissions Committee has completed its review of your application and would like to invite you to be on the waiting list. A small number of top candidates for admission to the 2016 entering class are invited to be on the waiting list.

Please contact Brandi Saunders in the admissions office by email  if you do not want to be placed on the waiting list.

As the application review process progresses, the Admissions Committee will periodically offer admission to candidates who are on the waiting list. Since the review process is ongoing, it is not possible to know when candidates from the waiting list will be admitted. Some candidates may be admitted after only a week or two on the waiting list, and some candidates may be on the list for a longer period of time.

Please note that there is no individual ranking of candidates on the waiting list and the size of the waiting list is not disclosed. All candidates on the waiting list will be evaluated for admission if places in the entering class become available.

Please let us know if you have questions or if you need additional information.

Sincerely,

Ramsey Bridges

Ramsey Bridges
Director of Law Admissions

Athens, Georgia 30602-6012
Telephone 706-542-5188 • Telefax 706-542-5556 • www.law.uga.edu
An Equal Opportunity/Affirmative Action/Veteran/Disability Institution

APPENDIX J: ACCEPTANCE LETTERS

April 15 2016

Dear Aram:

Thank you for your interest in SMU Dedman School of Law. After a careful review of your application, the Admissions Committee would like to offer you a place on our waitlist. Each year the number of qualified applicants to SMU Dedman School of Law greatly exceeds the number of available seats in the first-year class. As a result, the Admissions Committee is simply unable to offer admission to all applicants who possess the qualifications necessary to become a successful law student at SMU.

Please notify the Office of Admissions if you do not wish to remain on the wait list by clicking here. Statements of continued interest may be submitted by clicking here and will be added to your application for the Admissions Committee's consideration. Phone messages and drop-in visits are less effective.

Please keep your contact information up-to-date, as we may need to contact you quickly in the event that a seat becomes available. Applicants on the waitlist are not ranked and we are unable to tell you what your "chances" are to be admitted.

Please contact us if you have any questions or concerns.

Sincerely,

Jill Nikirk

Assistant Dean for Admissions

LSAT NECESSARY: An LSAT Prep Test Guide for the Non-logical Thinker

SCHOOL of LAW

March 21, 2016

Dear Aram,

We sincerely appreciate your interest in the Wake Forest University School of Law. After careful consideration of your application we remain interested in your candidacy and are impressed by the obvious talent and relevant experience you possess. At this time we have placed your application on our waitlist.

We hope that you will view this as a positive development. As we proceed through the application review process and the composition of the applicant pool and the incoming class take shape we'll revisit the waitlist. In order to make further decisions on waitlisted applications we'll take into consideration any additional information you submit to us.

We ask that you update us immediately if your interest or contact information changes. Before an offer of admission is made we will contact you by email or phone to discuss the opportunity. If we are unable to contact you, time constraints demand that we move on to other interested candidates.

We understand that the waitlist can be a stressful place to be and strive to provide information to alleviate your anxiety. Obviously, you are a candidate of considerable talent. The strength and size of the applicant pool this year have made it exceptionally competitive and by gaining a spot on the waitlist you've already distinguished yourself.

Thank you for your patience with our admission process. Do not hesitate to contact us if you have questions or would like to submit additional information.

Warmest regards,

R. Jay Shively, J.D. '99
Dean for Admissions and Financial Aid

APPENDIX J: ACCEPTANCE LETTERS

March 24, 2016

Dear Mr. Shah,

The Admissions Committee has completed the initial review of your application for admission to the fall 2016 entering class. The Committee was impressed with your application and would like to place you on our waitlist. Due to the large number of applications we receive and the fact that we have a small entering class, we must utilize a waitlist. The Committee is asking you for more time to consider your application, so we are hopeful you will allow us to place you on our waitlist.

Decisions will be made on an ongoing basis throughout the spring and summer, and we will provide you with regular updates on the status of your application through the Applicant Status Online and by email. If you remain interested in Colorado Law, we ask that you go to ~~[redacted]~~ and **complete the Continued Interest Form by April 15, 2016.**

You are welcome to submit **new** information that was not included in your original application via email attachment to law.admissions@colorado.edu. Examples of new information include: updates to your résumé, new honors, awards or acknowledgements, new academic information, and/or new letters of recommendation.

Financial aid will remain available to students offered admission at any time, including from the waitlist. All applicants admitted off the waitlist will be considered for scholarship money. Financial aid at the University of Colorado Law School may include Federal Direct Unsubsidized Stafford loans, Federal Graduate PLUS loans, and private loans. Visit our web site at www.colorado.edu/law/admissions/financialaid/ for *Financial Aid Basics* designed to acquaint you with the financial aid process.

Thank you again for your interest in Colorado Law. In the meantime, please let us know if you have any questions.

Sincerely,

Kristine M. Jackson
Assistant Dean of Admissions and Financial Aid

University of Colorado Law School
Wolf Law Building, 403 UCB | Boulder, CO 80309
Phone: (303) 492-7203 | Fax: (303) 492-2542
E-mail | Website | CU News

Levin College of Law

03/24/2016

Mr. Aarambh M. Shah

Dear Mr. Shah:

Thank you for your application to the University of Florida Levin College of Law. We have reviewed your application and are offering you a place on our wait list. Waitlisted applicants have clearly demonstrated the ability to succeed at UF Law, and may be offered a seat on a space-available basis anytime between now and the first day of Orientation (August 9, 2016). Please note, however, that it is impossible to predict when or if a particular applicant will be admitted.

We understand that you are likely to have questions about how our waitlist process works and what this offers means for you. Please review the attached Wait List FAQ's and do not hesitate to contact Noemar Castro, Ian McInnis, or me with further questions.

If you wish to remain on the wait list, please complete and return the attached form as soon as possible. We must receive your form *no later than Monday, April 11, 2016 by 5pm EST*.

We appreciate your interest in the University of Florida Levin College of Law.

Sincerely yours,

Grant W. Keener

Interim Assistant Dean for Admissions

APPENDIX J: ACCEPTANCE LETTERS

 University of California, Irvine

Admissions and
Student Financial Services

May 4, 2016

Mr. Aarambh M. Shah
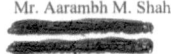

Dear Mr. Shah:

    We have completed a thorough review of your application and at this time you have been placed on our wait list for the entering class of fall 2016. You should not view this as an unfavorable outcome, as we recognize the merits of your candidacy. However, in keeping with our aspiration to maintain an environment that is framed by a uniquely low student-to-faculty ratio, placing a value on enrollment outcomes is important to us.

    I anticipate that we will review our wait list, which is unranked, beginning later this spring and continue as needed until the beginning of classes in August. Unfortunately, we cannot predict the likelihood or timing of acceptance, if it is forthcoming.

    If you wish to accept our offer of wait list status, you need to do nothing other than keep us informed of changes to your contact information or provide updates such as spring grades, awards and honors at graduation, or any other recent endeavors. If you would like to forward an update for inclusion in your application file or if you no longer wish to be considered for the upcoming entering class, please contact us directly via email at admissions@law.uci.edu and we will make the appropriate modifications per your request.

    Thank you for your patience during this process.

Warm regards,

Janice L. Austin

Janice L. Austin
Assistant Dean
Admissions and Student Financial Services

School of Law
401 East Peltason Drive, Irvine, CA 92697-8000
(949) 824-4545 | admissions@law.uci.edu

www.law.uci.edu

Index

0-100 Scoring 12–16
15-Point triage rule 176–177
    Logic games 181–183
    Logical reasoning 184–188
    Reading comprehension 177–181
180 Score 6, 169–170, 192
6 Month study plan 132–135

Ability 4, 9–10, 169–170, 195–199
Acceptance letters 192, 232–242
Admissions process 229–231
Accompanying, logic games 149–153
Adjectives 73, 220
Admissions, law school 6, 229–231
Adverbs 73, 104–105
Advertising example 60–65
"A-ha" moments 51, 65, 131, 196
'All' statements 13–14
    Deductive reasoning 46–47
    Inference questions 97, 99
    Passive patterns 83, 85
Analogy questions 99–101
Analytical reasoning: *see* Logic games
'And', Sufficiency vs. necessity 25–26
Answer choices
    Common traps 227–228
    Evaluate questions 117

Finding the truth 12–13
Flaw questions 111–112
Guessing 180–181, 186
Inference questions 98–99, 127
Logic games 139, 142
Logical reasoning questions
    162–163
Main-point-conclusion questions
    105–106
'Most Strongly Support'
    questions 100–101
Necessary assumption questions
    119
Parallel flaw questions 112,
    112–113
Parallel reasoning questions 113,
    114
Point-at-issue questions 109–110
Practice 135
Principle example questions
    103–104
Principle questions 114–115
Reading comprehension 129, 130
Resolve/ explain questions
    101–102
Reviewing practice tests 174
Strategy role questions 107

INDEX

Strategy technique questions 108
Strengthen questions 116
Sufficient assumption questions 118
Weaken questions 117
Anticipations: *see* Predictions
Appeal to authority 39–40
Applications, law school 6, 229–231
Argument structures 37–45, 92
Arguments
    Evidence 74–76
    Logical reasoning questions 92–96, 161–163
    Non-related arguments 54–59
    Reading comprehension 123, 222–223
    'Related but on steroids' 60–66
    Skills 10–11
    Validity 21–22
Assumption questions 3–4, 18, 93, 117–119
Assumptions
    Attacking the assumption 40–41, 54, 192
    Discovering your assumption 89
    Logical reasoning questions 54, 95–96, 162
    Non-related arguments 54–59
    'Related but on steroids' arguments 60–66
    Selective reasoning 38–42
    Strengthen questions 115
    Valid statements 78–81
Attacking the questions, logic games 157–158
AVB Opinions 109

Background, prior to law 1–2, 6
Background information
    Logical reasoning questions 94–95
    Reading comprehension 221
    Selective reasoning 38

Beach example 39–41
Best practice: *see* Strategy
Big picture questions, reading comprehension 126–127, 128, 178–180, 217
Billboards example 60–65
Blind guessing strategy 180–181
Block method, patterns 82–89
Business model, law schools 6, 68–69, 192
Business thinking
    Background prior to law 10
    LSAT comparison to 168–169, 172
    Sales techniques 40, 43, 160, 168

'Cannot Be True': *see* 'Must Be False'
Capability 4, 9–10, 169–170, 195–199
Casting doubt 91, 116–117
Cat example 49–51, 84–85
Categorical statements 13
see also Universal statements
Causal arguments
    Correlation vs. causation 33–35, 63–64, 112
    'Home-wrecker' analogy 32–33, 61, 64
    'Married Couple' analogy 31–32, 61, 64
    Strengthen questions 115
Cause and effect 31–35
Chained rules 97–98, 143, 147–149
Chart sketches 152–153
Choosing, logic games 143–149
Chunking strategy 184–185
Circular reasoning 111–112
Claims, 'Related but on steroids' 60, 63–64
Coffee example 13–14
Coincidence 32, 33, 34, 64
Common knowledge 39
Common patterns: *see* Passive patterns

249

Comparative passages 129–130
Comped tuition fees 6, 68–69, 192
Comprehension: *see* Reading
   comprehension
Conclusions 104–106
   Cause and effect 33–35
   Common patterns 200–203
   Logical reasoning questions
      95–96, 161–162
   Main-point-conclusion questions
      104–106
   No Valid Conclusion 82, 84
   Non-related arguments 54–59
   Passive patterns 69–74, 76–77,
      82–86, 88–89
   Reading comprehension 122
   'Related but on steroids' 60–66
   Selective reasoning 37–41, 42–44
Conditional statements: *see* If-Then
   conditional statements
Contrapositive
   Assumptions 57, 62
   Logic games 145–146
   Passive patterns 86
   Sufficiency vs. necessity 20–21,
      24–25, 26–27, 28, 30
Control: *see* Taking control
Correlation vs. causation 33–35,
   63–64, 112
'Could Be False' 14–16
   Deductive reasoning 48
   If-Then conditional statements
      20–21
   Lawyers' role 22
'Could Be True' 14–16
   Deductive reasoning 47–48
   If-Then conditional statements
      20–21
   Lawyers' role 22
   Logic games 141, 142, 155–156
   Sufficiency vs. necessity 29
Counterexamples 44, 61, 75
Critical thinking 4, 7–8, 59

Criticism: *see* Flaws
CrossFit example 70

Data, selective reasoning 45
Decision-making 176
Deductive reasoning 43–44, 46–53
   Logic games 154–156, 158
   see also Inference questions
   Definitions, reading
      comprehension 124
Dependency, sufficiency vs. necessity
   17–18
   see also Assumptions
Details, reading comprehension 124,
   127–128, 178–180, 217–218
Diet Coke example 71–72
Difficult questions: *see* Hard questions
Discovering your assumption 89
Discrepancies
   Logical reasoning questions
      93–94
   Resolve/ explain questions
      101–102
Distributing, logic games 149–153,
   213–215
Doubt, casting 91, 116–117
Duplicate words 77–80, 96, 97, 127,
   156

Easy questions 118, 171–172, 181–182,
   183, 186
Effect, cause and 31–35
Equivocation 112
Errors: *see* Flaws
Evaluate questions 117
Events, cause and effect 31
Evidence
   Common patterns 200–203
   Logical reasoning questions
      95–96, 161–162
   Non-related arguments 54–59
   Passive patterns 71–72, 74–81
   Reading comprehension 122

INDEX

'Related but on steroids' 60-66
Selective reasoning 36-37, 38, 40-44
Except questions 127-128
Explain, reading comprehension 123, 221-222
Explain/ resolve questions 101-102
Extreme answer choices 93, 98, 105, 163, 218, 227

Facts
    Inference questions 99
    Logical reasoning questions 92, 93-94, 96
    'Most Strongly Support' questions 100
'False' statements 14-16
Ferrari example 70
Finding the truth 12-16, 42, 46-53
First sentences 169, 178-179
Flaw questions 110-112
    Parallel flaw questions 112-113
    Resolve/ explain questions 102
Flaws
    Assumptions 58-59, 66, 89
    Types of question 90, 110-113
Formal logic conclusions 72, 73

Gambler analogy 189-190
Generalizing
    Assumptions 58
    Deductive reasoning 47
    Principle example questions 102-104
    Principle questions 114
    Selective reasoning 44
Grouping I games 140, 143-149, 210-213
Grouping II games 140, 149-151, 213-215
Guessing
    Logic games 183
    Logical reasoning questions 186

Reading comprehension 127, 179, 180-181
Skipping questions 134
Guilty by association 84

Hangman sketches 141, 153
Hard questions
    Logic games 183
    Main point mantra 185-187
    Reading comprehension 177, 179
    Skipping 159, 171
    Taking control 176-177
    Timing 198
Hedging words 31, 70, 113
'Home-wrecker' analogy 32-35, 61, 64
Hybrid games 140, 153-156

If-Then conditional statements
    Logic games 144
    Passive patterns 72
    Principle example questions 103
    Principle questions 114
    Sufficiency vs. necessity 17, 18-20, 23, 25-29
In-and-out sketches 147-149
Inductive reasoning 44
Inference questions
    If-Then conditional statements 29
    Passive patterns 82
    Reading comprehension 127, 178-180, 218
    Strategy 3, 93-94, 96, 97-99
    Wording 72
Inferences
    Deductive reasoning 46-53
    Logic games 146-147
Inputs, selective reasoning 45
Instant gratification 170, 173, 189
Internalizing information 6-7

Keywords 5
    and Conclusions 73-74

251

Evaluate questions 117
Flaw questions 110
Inference questions 97
Logical reasoning questions 95
Main-point-conclusion questions 104–105
'Most Strongly Support' questions 99
Necessary assumption questions 118
Ordering games 140
Parallel flaw questions 112–113
Point-at-issue questions 108
Principle example questions 102
Principle questions 114
Reading comprehension 123–124, 126, 220–221
Resolve/ explain questions 101
Strategy role questions 106
Strategy technique questions 107–108
Strengthen questions 115
Sufficient assumption questions 117
Weaken questions 116

Lamborghini example 16–17, 24, 25–26, 30
Language of lawyers 23, 193–194
Law schools
    Admissions 6, 229–231
    Scholarships 6, 68–69, 192
    Skills 170–171
Lawyers' role
    'Could Be True' 22
    Language 11, 23, 193–194
    Selective reasoning 41–42
Level-of-certainty 74
Logic 1
Logic games 137–139
    15-Point triage rule 181–183
    Attacking the questions 157–158
    Grouping I games 140, 143–149

Grouping II games 140, 149–151
Hybrid games 140, 153–156
If-Then conditional statements 28
Inference questions 97–98
Matching games 140, 151–153
Ordering games 140–143
Practice 138–139, 159, 181, 204–216
Scripts 161
Skipping questions 154, 158–159, 161, 182
Sufficiency vs. necessity 18, 24, 147
Types of 140
Logical opposites 15–16, 50, 52
Logical reasoning questions 5
    15-Point triage rule 184–188
    Assumptions 54, 58, 65
    Importance of 88–89
    Paraphrasing 94–96
    Reading comprehension 219
    Scripts 161–163
    Selective reasoning 36–45
    Skipping questions 186, 187, 188
    Strategy 10, 92–94
    see also Inference questions; Strategy
Longer questions 195–197
Loose ordering 140, 142–143
Loose sequencing 208–210
'Lost in the sauce' analogy 37, 123
LR: *see* Logical reasoning questions
LSAT, passing the test 191–192, 224–226
    see also Test day
LSAT mastery 10–11, 59, 191–192, 196
Luxury brands example 54–59

Main point mantra 185–187
Main points, reading comprehension 126–127, 128, 164–165

INDEX

Main-point-conclusion questions 104–106, 190
Major skills, lawyers 10–11, 12, 170–171, 193–194
Marathon example 67–68
Marking up passages 123, 124, 125–126
'Married Couple' analogy 31–32, 61, 64
Maslow's hierarchy of needs 11
Mastery example 59
Mastery of LSAT 10–11, 59, 191–192, 196
Matching games 140, 151–153, 215–216
Measuring improvement 160–161
Memory, of passages
    Inference questions 99
    Reading comprehension 122, 129, 165
Mental exhaustion 9
Million-dollar game 167–168
'Missing links' 89
    see also Assumptions
Mistaken negation 17, 21
Mistaken reversal 19–20, 21
Modifiers 220
'Most are not' statements 13, 14
'Most' statements 13, 14
    Deductive reasoning 49–50
    Passive patterns 82–84, 86–87
    Strengthen questions 115
    Weaken questions 116
'Most Strongly Support' questions 99–101
Multiple choice 12–13
    see also Answer choices
Multiple sketches, logic games 137–139, 141–142
Murder case example 91
'Must Be False' 14–16
    Deductive reasoning 48
    Logic games 141, 156, 157–158

Strategy 97–99
'Must Be True' 14–16, 192
    Block method 86–88
    Deductive reasoning 47–48
    Evidence 74–75, 76
    If-Then conditional statements 20–21
    Logic games 141, 142, 147, 149, 155–156, 157–158
    Strategy 97–99
    Sufficiency vs. necessity 29
    Valid statements 25–27
Mutual exclusivity 48–49, 50, 65

Natural ability 4, 9–10, 169–170, 195–199
Necessary assumption questions 18, 93, 118–119
Necessary conditions 17, 24, 26–29
Necessary terms 17–18, 23–24, 77–80
    see also Sufficiency vs. necessity
Negating terms 17, 21
Negative words 61–62
'No' statements 48–49
No Valid Conclusion (NVC) 82, 84
'None' statements 13–14
Non-related arguments 54–59
'Not' (negatives) 61–62
'Not all' statements 13, 14
'Not both' rule, logic games 145–146, 150, 156
Note-taking, reading comprehension 123–124, 125–126
Nouns 221
NVC (No Valid Conclusion) 82, 84

Olympic long-jumper analogy 42–45
    Assumptions 54, 55, 60, 62, 65–66
    Common patterns 200–203
    Types of question 90–91
Opinions
    Conclusions 73

253

Keywords 220
Logical reasoning questions 94
Main-point-conclusion questions 105
Point-at-issue questions 109–110
Selective reasoning 38–39
'Or'
  Logic games 145, 150
  Sufficiency vs. necessity 24–26
Order of questions: *see* Skipping questions
Ordering games 140–143, 205–210
Outputs, selective reasoning 45
Overlooked possibilities 110

Parallel flaw questions 112–113
Parallel reasoning questions 113–114
Paraphrasing 5, 94–96
Particular statements
  Assumptions 57–58
  Deductive reasoning 46, 49–50, 52
  Passive patterns 88
  see also 'Could Be False'; 'Could Be True'; 'Some' statements
Passages, reading comprehension 121–123, 129–130, 163–164, 220–223
Passing the test 191–192, 224–226
Passive patterns
  Block method 82–89
  Conclusions 69–74, 200–203
  Evidence 74–76, 200–203
  Flaw questions 110–111
  Marathon example 67–69
  Sufficient assumptions 78–81
  Valid statements 76–78
  Wrong answers 227–228
Past vs. future 64–65
Perfect scores 6, 192
Point made questions 104–106
Point-at-issue questions 108–110

see also headings beginning Main point
Points: *see* Scores, LSAT
Polar opposites 16
Police investigation example 91
'Possible' statements 14–16
Practice
  Arguments 95–96
  Importance of 8–9, 131–132, 191
  Logic games 138–139, 159, 181, 204–216
  Marathon example 67–68
  Measuring improvement 160–161
  and Scores 4
  Six-month study plan 132–135
  Timing 132–134, 135–136, 199
  see also Strategy
Practice tests (PT) 3, 5
Prep tests 5, 134–135, 174
Reviewing 135, 173–175
Predicates 221
Predictions
  Flaw questions 111
  Parallel flaw questions 113
  Parallel reasoning questions 113
  Passive patterns 70, 73
  Reading comprehension 126
Premises
  Cause and effect 33
  Deductive reasoning 52
  Parallel flaw questions 112
  Passive patterns 82–83
Prep tests 5, 134–135, 174
  see also Practice tests
Prepping: *see* Practice
Prescriptions 62–63
  Passive patterns 70–71, 73
Presuppositions: *see* Assumptions
Principle example questions 102–104
Principle questions 114–115
Profitability example 54–59
PT: *see* Practice tests

INDEX

Purpose, reading comprehension 123
Push-up method, reading comprehension 125, 220

Qualifiers
    Conclusions 112-113
    Evidence 71-72, 74
    Keywords 220
    Logic games 145-146
    Strengthening/ weakening 89, 115, 116
Quantities 86, 89
    0-100 Scoring 13-16
Question types: *see* Types of question

Ranking, logic games 140-143
Rankings, law schools 6, 69, 230-231
Readiness for test 224-226
Reading comprehension (RC) 121-130
    15-Point triage rule 177-181
    Scripts 163-166
    Skipping questions 129, 177, 179
    Structure patterns 220-223
    Types of question 217-219
Red Bull example 18-19, 24, 118, 119
'Related but on steroids' arguments 60-66, 89, 119
Relationships, sufficiency vs. necessity 22
Relative comparison 71-72, 73
Researching, reading comprehension 121-122
Resolve/ explain questions 101-102
Results: *see* Passing the test; Scores, LSAT
Reverse "U" patterns 81, 93
Reversing terms 19-20, 21
Reviewing practice tests 135, 173-175
Revisiting book 7
Roles, strategy role questions 106-107, 184
Rolex example 54-59

Roster sketches 151, 152
Rule on the bottom questions 102-104
Rule on top questions 114-115
Rule-eliminator questions 157

Sales techniques 40, 43, 160, 168
Scanning, reading comprehension 123-124, 127
Scheduling, logic games 140-143
Scholarships 6, 68-69, 192
Scores, LSAT
    180 LSAT Score 6, 169-170, 192
    Million-dollar game 167-168
    Passing the test 191
    and Practice 4
    Strategy 167, 168-169, 171-172
    Timing 169-171
Scoring words, 0-100 scale 12-16
Scripts 160-161
    Logic games 161
    Logical reasoning 161-163
    Reading comprehension 163-166
Selecting, logic games 143-149, 210-213
Selective reasoning 36-45
Self-actualization, Maslow's hierarchy of needs 11
Sequencing, logic games 140-143, 205-210
Shirt example 19-21
'Should' 62-63
'Should not' 62-63
Signs of readiness for test 224-226
Single-action games 181-182
Sketches, logic games 137-139
    Grouping I games 144, 146, 147-149
    Grouping II games 151
    Hybrid games 154-156
    Matching games 152-153
    Ordering games 141-142

255

Skills, of lawyers 10–11, 12, 170–171, 193–194
Skipping questions
    Logic games 154, 158–159, 161, 182
    Logical reasoning questions 186, 187, 188
    Reading comprehension 129, 177, 179
    Strategies 168, 169, 171–172, 174–175
    Timing 133, 134, 185–187, 195–197
Soft assumptions 93, 118, 119
'Some are not' statements 13, 14
'Some' statements 13, 14
    Deductive reasoning 49–50
    Passive patterns 82–84, 85, 86
'Something needed' 220
Speed 59
    see also Timing
Spider web sketches 141
Stack sketches, logic games 153–154
Stacked sentences 38
Statistics, selective reasoning 45
'Steroids', 'related but on' arguments 60–66, 89, 119
Stimulus structure, logical reasoning 92, 94–95, 96
Strategy
    Book's purpose 5–11
    Evaluate questions 117
    Flaw questions 110–112
    Inference questions 97–99
    Logic games 137–139, 161, 181–183
    Logical reasoning questions 90–96, 119–120, 161–163, 184–188
    Main-point-conclusion questions 104–106
    'Most Strongly Support' questions 99–101

'Must Be True' questions 157
Necessary assumption questions 118–119
Parallel flaw questions 112–113
Parallel reasoning questions 113–114
Paraphrasing 94–96
Point-at-issue questions 108–110
Practice 131–132
Principle example questions 102–104
Principle questions 114–115
Reading comprehension 121–130, 163–166, 177–181, 217–219
Resolve/ explain questions 101–102
Rule-eliminator questions 157
Scoring 167, 168–169, 171–172
Scripts 161–166
Six-month study plan 132–135
Strategy role questions 106–107
Strategy technique questions 107–108
Strengthen questions 115–116
Sufficient assumption questions 18, 93, 117–118
Weaken questions 116–117
    see also Guessing; Skipping questions; Timing
Strategy role questions 106–107
Strategy technique questions 107–108
Strengthen questions 115–116
Strengthen/ weaken arguments 31–34, 41–42, 45, 58–59, 90–91
Stress 133, 159, 174
Strict hangman sketches 141–142
Strict ordering 140
Structure, reading comprehension 220–223
Structure of arguments 37–45, 92
Study guides 1
Studying example 31, 32–33

INDEX

Sub-conclusions 38, 105–106
Subjects (as keyword) 221
Sufficiency vs. necessity 16–22
    Logic games 18, 24, 147
    Wording 22–30
Sufficient assumption questions
    Keywords 22–24
    Passive patterns 77, 78–81
    Strategy 18, 93, 117–118
Sufficient conditions 17, 24–25, 27–30
Supports most strongly questions 99–101

Taking control 176–177, 179, 184–185
Target scores 4, 6, 169–170
T-charts 109, 116, 145
Terminology: *see* Wording
Test day 1–3, 133, 134–135, 176–177, 189–191
Thinking about logic games 161
Thinking critically 4, 7–8, 59
    see also Passive patterns
Three-minute rule 128–129
Timing
    Abilities 169–170, 198–199
    Conclusions 72–74
    Importance of 2–3, 4
    Logic games 138–139, 158–159, 181
    Logical reasoning questions 59
    Longer questions 195–197
    Practice 132–134, 135–136
    Reading comprehension 123–124, 128–129, 130
    and Scoring 169–171
    Skipping questions 133, 134, 185–187, 195–197
Training, Marathon example 67–68
Trap answers: *see* Wrong answers
Tricks of the trade: *see* Strategy
Triggers
    Assumptions 62
    Cause and effect 33

Logic games 147
    Sufficiency vs. necessity 28–29
'True' statements 14–16
Truth finding 12–16, 87
Tuition discounts 6, 68–69, 192
Types of logic games 139, 140
Types of question, logical reasoning 90–91
    see also Skipping questions; Strategy
Types of question, reading comprehension 217–219
Typing out arguments 95

"U" patterns 80–81, 93
Underlining, reading comprehension 123–124, 125–126
Universal statements 13–14
    Assumptions 57–58
    Conclusions 77
    Deductive reasoning 52
    If-Then conditional statements 20–21
    Inference questions 97
    Passive patterns 85, 88
    Selective reasoning 43–44
    Sufficient assumption questions 118
    see also 'All' statements; 'Must Be False'; 'Must Be True'
'Unless', sufficiency vs. necessity 29–30
'Until', sufficiency vs. necessity 29–30
U.S. News and World Report 6, 69

Valid statements 21–22
    Passive patterns 76–78
    Sufficiency vs. necessity 25–27
Verbs 221
Viewpoints
    Conclusions 73
    Main-point-conclusion questions 106

Reading comprehension
   122–123
Selective reasoning 37–38
Strategy role questions 106–107
Waiting lists, law school 229–231
Weak predictions 113
Weaken questions 116–117
Weaken/ strengthen arguments
   31–34, 41–42, 45, 58–59, 90–91
What if scenarios 29, 42, 157–158
What if sketches 137–138
'Why'
   Conclusions 95, 105
   Evidence 37, 40, 162
   Reading comprehension
      124–125
'Without', sufficiency vs. necessity
   29–30
Word documents 95
Wording
   0-100 scoring 12–16
   Assumptions 60–61
   Conclusions 70–71, 72, 73, 74
   Finding the truth 13
   Hedging words 31, 70, 113
   Main-point-conclusion questions
      104–106
   Negatives 61–62

Selective reasoning 38
Sufficiency vs. necessity 22–30
see also Keywords
Wrong answers 3–4
   Common traps 227–228
   Evaluate questions 117
   Flaw questions 111–112
   Inference questions 98–99, 127
   Main-point-conclusion questions
      105–106
   'Most Strongly Support'
      questions 100–101
   Necessary assumption questions
      119
   Parallel flaw questions 113
   Parallel reasoning questions 114
   Point-at-issue questions 110
   Principle example questions
      103–104
   Principle questions 114–115
   Resolve/ explain questions 102
   Strategy role questions 107
   Strategy technique questions 108
   Strengthen questions 116
   Sufficient assumption questions
      118
   Weaken questions 117

ABOUT THE AUTHOR

Aarambh "Aram" Shah is a business entrepreneur turned LSAT connoisseur. After starting, scaling, and selling off several small businesses, Aram realized what was most important to him: pursuing a law degree. As a result, he has dedicated himself to helping students with little to no logical-reasoning background understand the LSAT from a rudimentary level to focus on what matters: scoring points.

Aram holds a Masters of Arts degree in Mass Communication and a Master of Science degree in Entrepreneurship from the University of Florida. Aram also holds a Master of Science degree in Real Estate Development from New York University.

www.ingramcontent.com/pod-product-compliance
Lightning Source LLC
Chambersburg PA
CBHW021430080526
44588CB00009B/489